CW01654300

SUGARCRAFT FLOWERS

Through the Four Seasons

SPRING

Rosemary Merrills

Bramble Books

This book is dedicated to Rita Miller, who taught me basic sugar flowers, and whose enthusiasm and skill inspired me to continue.

Also my friends Carolyn, Hazel, Ann and Joyce, with whom I have shared many hours of fun and, occasionally, a sugarcraft idea or two.

PUBLISHED IN 1993 BY
ROSEMARY MERRILLS
OLD FARM LODGE,
LAMBERHURST QUARTER,
TUNBRIDGE WELLS,
KENT TN3 8AR.

DESIGNED BY BOB BICKERTON

PHOTOGRAPHY BY RODDY PAINE

TYPESET AND PRINTED BY
THE LOWFIELD PRINTING COMPANY, DARTFORD, KENT

ISBN 0 9521323 0 3

All rights reserved. No part of this publication may be reproduced, stored in a retrieval system, or transmitted in any form or by any means, electronic, mechanical, photocopying, recording to otherwise, without prior written permission of the copyright owner.

CONTENTS

IMPORTANT NOTE

The drawings in this book are not to scale. In most cases they are larger than life. The exact measurements are given in the notes.

FOREWORD

Having admired Rosemary's work for several years, it gives me much pleasure to introduce her first book. I have found Rosemary to be a most gifted and artistic lady who pays meticulous attention to detail and presentation. She is an excellent demonstrator and the high quality of the work acheived by the students on her courses owes much to Rosemary's encouragement and patience as a tutor. Her methods of work are innovative and, in the best traditions of the Sugarcraft Guild, she readily shares with her students the results of hours of experimenting to gain perfection.

I hope that this book will bring Rosemary's skills to the attention of many more students and practitioners of Sugarcraft. Not only is this book with its beautiful photographs, a joy to look at but it is also a working manual with clear step by step instructions for making exquisite Spring flowers.

I look forward to forthcoming books on Summer, Autumn and Winter.

Eddie Spence

INTRODUCTION

It has been my pleasure and privilege to have lived all my life in the Garden of England. My favourite haunts are the country lanes and fields, where I can appreciate the natural beauty all around me. A longing to recreate these floral scenes in sugar, led me to develop new techniques for flower making, many of which you will find in this book.

In 1985, having completed a course in basic sugar flowers, I asked the question "Where do I go from here?" Three years later, in answer to this challenge, I developed a series of courses inspired by the four seasons. Themes under the separate titles: Spring, Summer, Autumn and Winter, have proved to be of great interest to my students, who have enjoyed many hours of creative work.

I hope that, through these pages, you will enjoy your journey into "SPRING".

Rosemary Merrills
Spring 1993

GLOSSARY

BODKIN Polished steel needle with a ball tip for threading ribbon. Use for cupping very small petals (see Lily of the Valley).

CONFECTIONER'S GLAZE Used for giving leaves a shiny finish. However, if used neat, the shine will be too hard. It is therefore necessary to break down the shellac content with alcohol:— To 100 mls of glaze, which should be re-potted into a wide-necked jar with a tight screw lid, add up to three teaspoons of Vodka or similar high-proof spirit (Gin is not high-proof enough). You must add one teaspoon at a time, shaking the liquid in between to prevent congealing.

FLOWER PARTS

PETALS:	Showy coloured parts which form the FLOWER.
SEPALS:	Usually coloured green, but sometimes the same colour as the petals. Together they form the CALYX, which protects the flower when in bud.
STAMENS:	A number of filaments with pollen-laden heads, found in the centre of the flower.
PISTIL:	Small stem (the STYLE) with a tip (the STIGMA) which is receptive to pollen. Found inside the stamens.

GROTTY BITS See LEAVES — BASIC METHOD.

GUNGE A very strong 'glue' made by breaking up tiny pieces of flower paste and dissolving it in Gin or Vodka (the alcohol prevents mixture going off). Use for repairs to broken petals etc., or for sticking difficult items (see Lilac).

HALF GLAZE See CONFECTIONER'S GLAZE.

HONITON BOBBIN A short wooden tool with a pointed end for making holes and a blunt end for rolling small petals. I don't know what I'd do without this!

LEAF VEINERS These can be purchased ready-made, or created from real leaves when in season. If using the latter, here is my own preferred method:—

Make an impression of the back of a real leaf on FIMO. This is a modelling agent available from most toy and model shops. Follow the instructions on the packet, but roll the FIMO out on a small piece of kitchen foil, so that it can be transferred to the oven without distortion.

NOTE: Occasionally you may get a better impression from the FRONT of a leaf. There is no hard and fast rule about this.

Having made a veiner of one side of a leaf, it is now possible to use this to make a veiner for the other side of a leaf, with LATEX VEINER-MAKER. This is usually available from Sugarcraft shops. The secret of successful Latex veiners is to brush the first coat onto the FIMO veiner very thinly, and make sure that you pop every bubble, however small. Leave to dry until the Latex changes from opaque white to clear, then add three or four further coats, allowing the Latex to dry in between each. Make these layers as thick as possible, without the Latex running off the edges. You now have a matching pair of veiners ready for use.

NOTE: It is possible to paint the Latex straight on to a real leaf, and then make a FIMO impression from this. It is a good idea to stick the real leaf to a card with double-sided tape to prevent curling up.

MEXICAN HAT A method for rolling out paste (brim) for the flower petals, with a small cone (crown) in the centre to hold stamens (see Periwinkle).

PAINT BRUSHES I suggest that you buy a small selection of good brushes, as these will make your powder colouring very much easier and more effective.

BRISTLE — Round, short head, used for brushing across the surface of twigs
FLAT: — Size 5/16ths inch wide, synthetic. Used for most petal colouring.
ROUND: — Sizes 00000 to 1 for fine line painting. Sable if possible
Sizes 3 to 5 for small delicate areas. Sable if possible

ROLLING PINS Do try to buy the non-stick variety if possible.
SIZE 1: — Very slim. About the thickness of size 11 knitting needles. Used for making the central vein in leaves and petals (see LEAVES)
SIZE 2: — Medium. About knitting needle size 3.
SIZE 3: — Large. Diameter 2.5 cms (1 inch).

SHADOW GREEN Powder colour used for shading the front of a leaf where no other colour is used. Mix Moss green and any other green with black until the mixture is as dark as required.

SKI STICKS A very useful way of twisting a wire to give maximum support. It can be used for wiring a small piece of paste for the centre of a flower or bud (see Apple Blossom). Also used for Acorns, Daisies and Rose Hips. NOTE: Use any wire up to and including 26 gauge. It is difficult to do the tight twist on a 24 gauge wire.

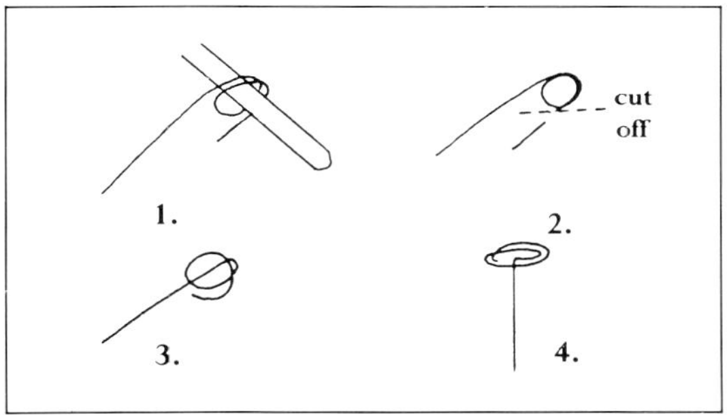

1. Twist wire round a small stick (a cocktail stick is rather small, but the size 1 rolling pin is about right for most occasions.
2. Cut off the short end of the wire.
3. Bend the wire 'disc' down over the long wire.
4. With the long wire on top, hold the 'disc' half way down with tweezers, and lift the long wire so that it is at right angles to the 'disc'. Now you can see why it's called a SKI STICK.

STAND FOR FLOWERS Some flowers look best when allowed to stand up as though they are growing naturally rather than arranged in a spray. In order to do this, use the wires from the flowers to make a small stand. Bind all the flowers and leaves together with fine silver wire just below the lowest growing point. Cover wire with tape. Divide the wires into three and tape down each group to the ends. Now bend the 'legs' out to form a tripod or ring. Alternatively, set the upright arrangement in a flower holder without bending the wire legs.

TAPESTRY NEEDLE (SIZE 13) A large polished steel needle with a blunt end, used for thinning and veining small petals and for opening up a small throat in the centre of a flower (see Lilac).

THROAT VEINERS Tools with five, six or eight 'splines' used for marking the throat of a flower (see Primrose).

WIRES PAPER COVERED: Used for supporting most flowers and leaves.
COTTON COVERED 'SCIENTIFIC' WIRE. On a spool. Very fine.
FINE SILVER UNCOVERED WIRE. Used for binding several stems together.

LEAVES – BASIC METHOD

The importance of well mades leaves in sugarcraft cannot be over emphasised. They will enhance your flowers and make them appear much more realistic.

The method described here has proved to be extremely effective. It eliminates the necessity to dry the leaf over a curved shape, because the wire, inserted almost to the tip, will support the leaf and allow it to be shaped whilst the paste is still soft.

Colour flower paste green — the lighter shade of the BACK of the real leaf, or, for autumn leaves, colour paste a warm cream.

For green leaves use green wires and for cream leaves use white wires.

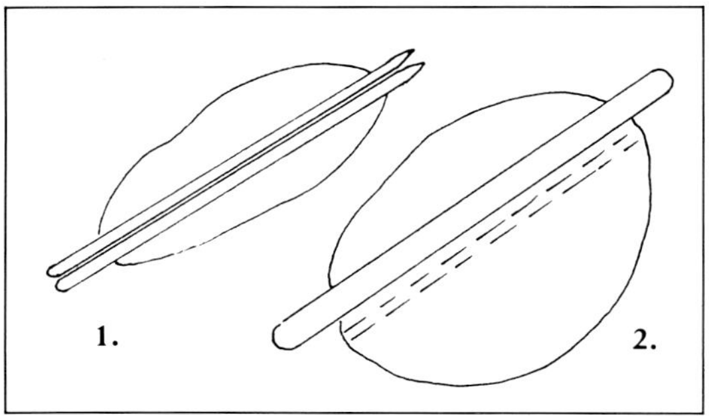

1. Roll out a small piece of paste to about 2mm (1/10th inch) thick, and as long as the cutter to be used. Place two very small (size 1) rolling pins side by side down the length of the paste and press firmly to make a narrow vein.

2. Using the next larger rolling pin (size 2), roll away the paste on either side of the vein, until very thin, and wide enough to fit the cutter.
Also thin away the paste at one end of the vein for about 5 mm (¼ inch).

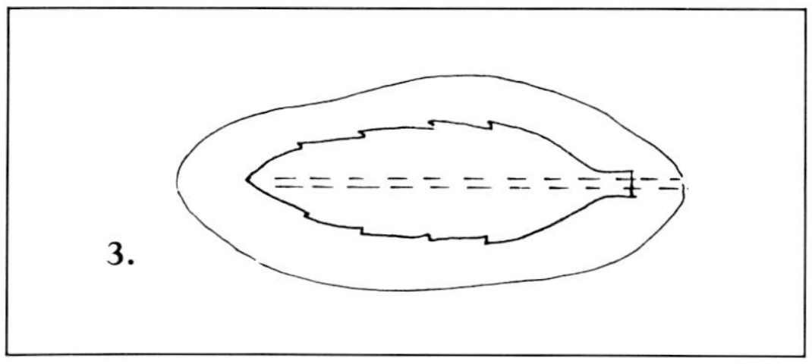

3. Place the cutter on the paste with the tip on the thinned away area (see 2) and the vein exactly down the middle.
Cut out the leaf cleanly.

4. Thin the edges of the leaf, but do not touch the vein.

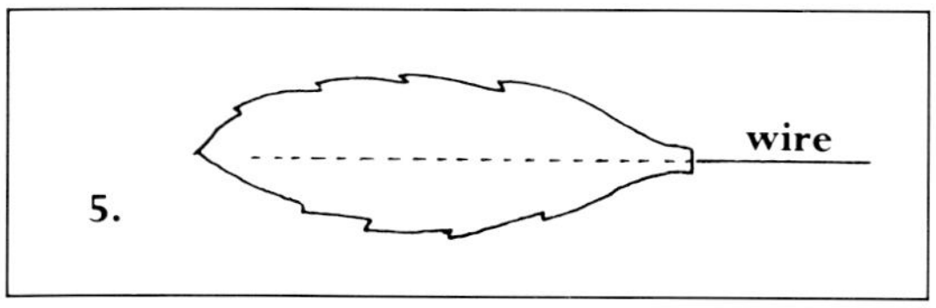

5. Holding the leaf carefully between the thumb and forefinger, insert a fine sewing needle into the lower end of the vein for about 2 cms (¾ inch). Remove needle and insert a 30 gauge wire, feeding it very slowly up into the leaf along the vein, until you reach the tip.
Press flat the along the vein to hold wire in.

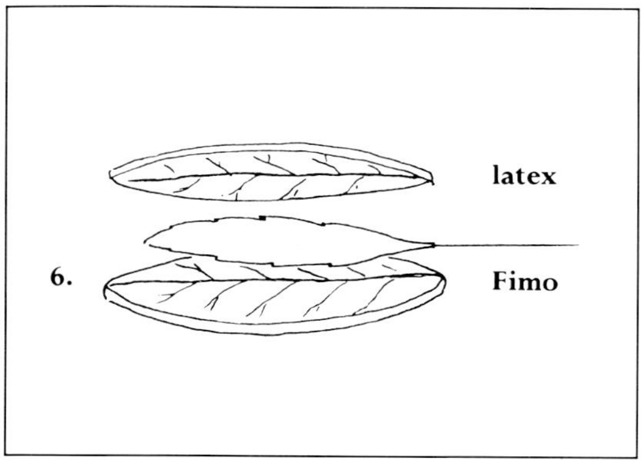

6. Lay leaf on the FIMO veiner with the middle of the leaf exactly in position down the central vein. Set the latex or top veiner in place and press firmly with even pressure all over.

7. Brush leaf with powder colours as required, using shadow green (see glossary) to darken the front of plain green leaves. Copy a real leaf or a good picture for detailed colouring. Don't forget to put colour on back of the leaf too.

8. Dip leaf completely into the half glaze (see glossary). Drain well, then blot very lightly between two layers of tissue.

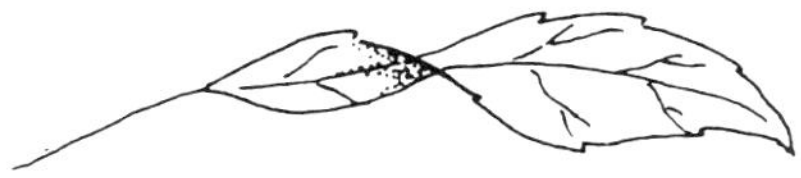

9.

9. Stand leaf in a holder for no more than five minutes. In normal drying conditions this will be long enough for the glaze to be absorbed into the paste, so that you can handle it.
Bend the wire to the required position, then curl and 'move' the leaf.

10. Stand the leaf again until completely dry.

"GROTTY BITS"

1/2.

1. To give your leaves character and to make them look old, create a few worm holes and 'chewed' edges.
Heat a large old darning needle in a flame until red hot, then push through the paste or along the edges as required. The carbon deposit will make the edges black.

2. The leaf may be speckled by sprinkling a few grains of the shadow green powder colour on to the freshly glazed surface, before blotting.

DEAD LEAVES

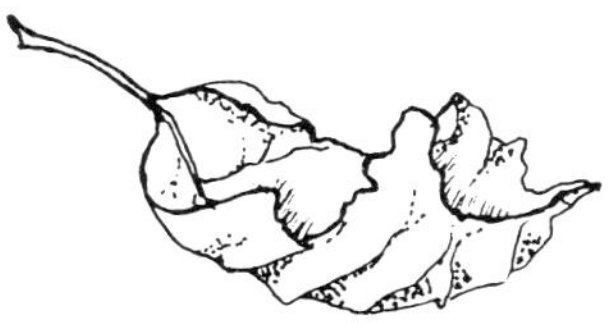

2/4.

1. Make leaves as above but use a brown base colour. Darken the colouring to dark brown, or as required.

2. After glazing, leave to dry for as short a time as possible, then crumple and curl the leaf.

3. With dark brown tape, cover 12 mm (½ inch) of the wire, thickening the tip.

4. Cut off at an angle, and curve the wire as shown.

IMPORTANT NOTE

The drawings in this book are not to sca e. In most cases they are larger than life. The exact measurements are given in the notes.

ANEMONE

Springtime's dawn, translucent light
Anemone, a jewel bright.
Down garden ways the first sweet showers
Make crystals of these lovely flowers.

Gaudily coloured anemones, or Wind Flowers as they are also known, are one of the most striking spring flowers, with their black stamens and furry centres. Very popular with flower arrangers, because they are so long lasting, they can be used as an equally dazzling arrangement on a celebration cake.

FLOWER

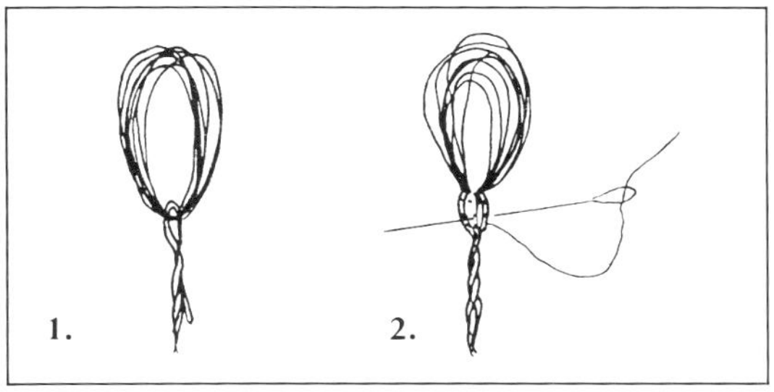

1. Prepare stamen centre: Twist black Sylko around one finger about 30 times. Hook a 30 gauge green wire through the loops and twist the wire very tightly about three or four times to hold the cottons securely.

2. Slip the loops from the finger. Thread Sylko onto a fine sewing needle and stitch through just above the wire to hold all the threads upright. (If you don't do this, they are inclined to separate into two halves).

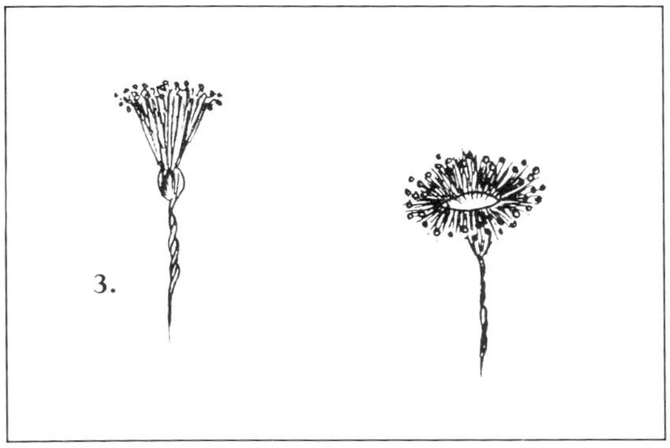

3. Trim the cottons to about 12mm (½ inch), then, holding them tightly, rub the tips with the rough side of an emery board. This will fluff out the threads so that they appear to be thicker.
Alternatively, put egg white onto the tips of the freshly trimmed cottons and dip into black Sugar Tex. Leave to dry.

4. Roll a very tiny ball of grey flower paste and press with the finger tip to flatten. Brush egg white carefully on one side only and drop into a small container in which you have mixed black Sugar Tex and white powder colour.
Leave this to dry until the flower is ready.

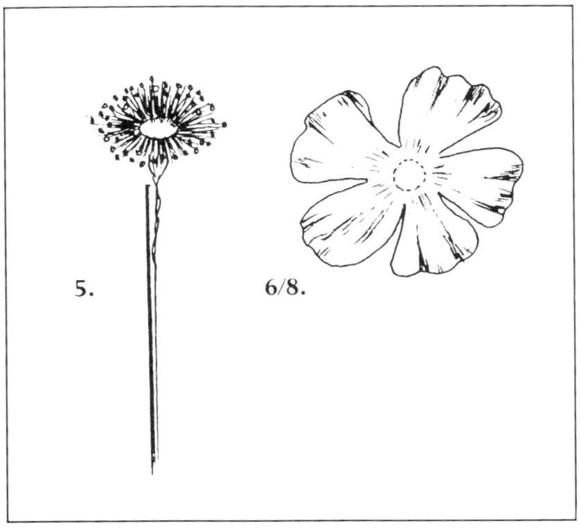

5. Tape in a 24 gauge green wire to strengthen the stem.

6. Roll out a small piece of white paste, not too thinly. Continue to roll round the edges, leaving a tiny 'pimple' of thicker paste in the centre, about 6mm (¼ inch) in diameter.

7. Cut out blossom flower, using an Orchard F7 cutter.
NB: Coloured paste may be used, but this will not allow you to have a white centre to your flower.

8. Using an Orchard non-stick balling tool, thin the edges of the petals until they are slightly fluted. Ball the centres to cup.

FLOWER

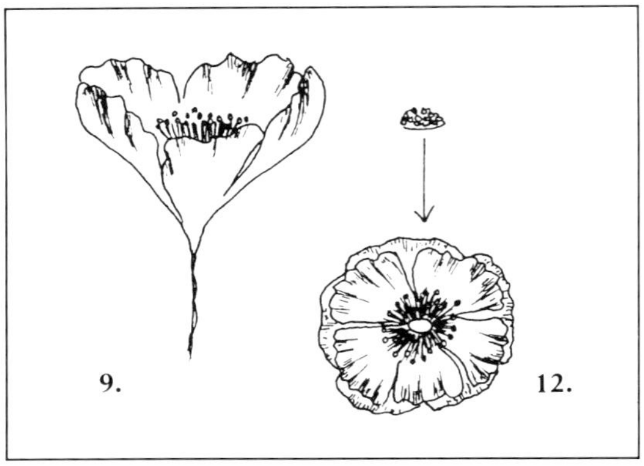

9. Make a small hole in the middle of the 'pimple' then pull through the cotton stamen centre until the knot disappears. At the same time, pinch the paste at the back to make a very small Mexican hat.

10. Leave to dry, then repeat with another petal, but omit the 'pimple' in the centre.

11. Once the petals are completely dry, brush with powder colour, using a flat brush and working in from the edges. Do not allow the colour to encroach into the white centre round the stamens.

12. Open up the stamen centre, put a dab of egg white into the middle and drop in the Sugar Tex grey centre. Press for a moment to ensure that it sticks, and holds the stamens open in a circle.

LEAVES

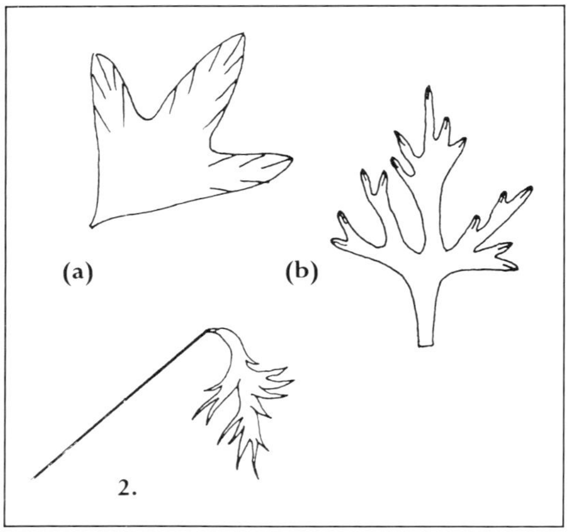

1. Colour flower paste a good fresh green. Cut out a ferny leaf, using one of the cutters illustrated.
If using cutter a) thin the edges, then snip all round as shown.
If using cutter b) make tiny cuts in the tip of each frond.
Press the tip of a Honiton bobbin firmly on each separate section to thin and spread.

2. Finish the leaves as shown on pages 10 & 11 using 30 gauge wires.
Colour the edges with a little yellow or cream powder and bend the wires as shown.

ASSEMBLY

1. Tape two leaves opposite each other, about $1\frac{1}{2}$ cms ($\frac{3}{5}^{ths}$ inch) below the flower.

2. Several flowers may be taped together, mixing the colours as required.

ANEMONE

APPLE BLOSSOM

Hear the buzzing of the bees
Amongst these blossom-laden trees,
It won't be long, as times goes by
Before I eat an apple pie.

Apple blossom is a very delicate and popular flower for celebration and wedding cakes. Create a really dramatic effect by adding a realistic bark effect to your branch.

CALYX

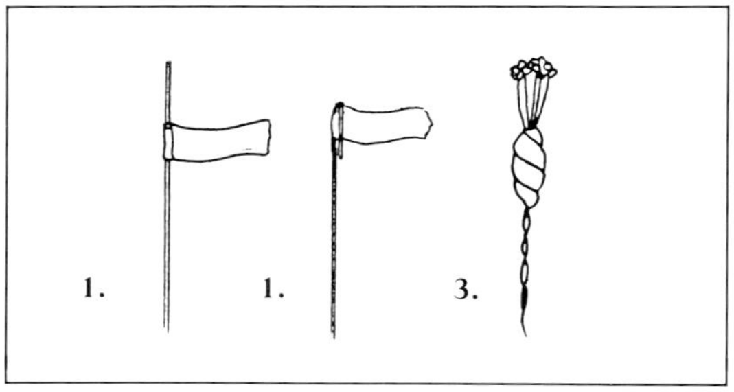

1. Prepare stamens: Join quarter-width green tape to 30 gauge green wire, about 6mm (¼ inch) below the tip. Bend the tip of the wire down over the tape.

2. Tape in 12 to 15 small cream irregular stamens, with their heads level about 7mm (3/10ths inch) above the tip of the wire, making a small fat pad with the tape.

3. Cut off the stamen cottons immediately below the pad and continue to tape down the wire for 3cms (1¼ inch). The stamens remain upright.

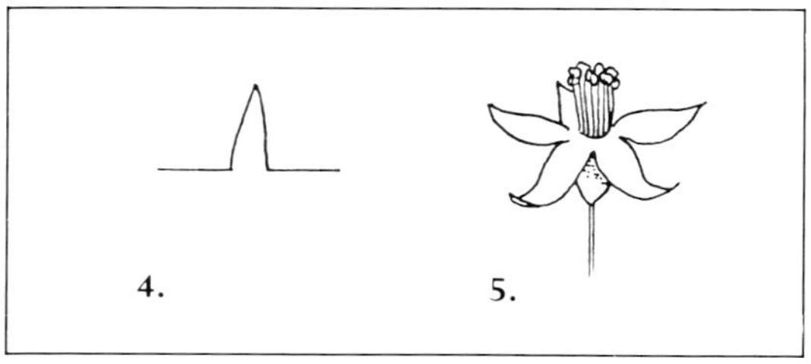

4. Colour flower paste apple green. Cut out the smallest calyx with a tiny Mexican hat. Thin the sepals a little.

5. Make a neat hole in the centre of the calyx and pull through the stamens until the pad of tape disappears down into the hole. Dry with the sepals slightly curved up.

PETALS

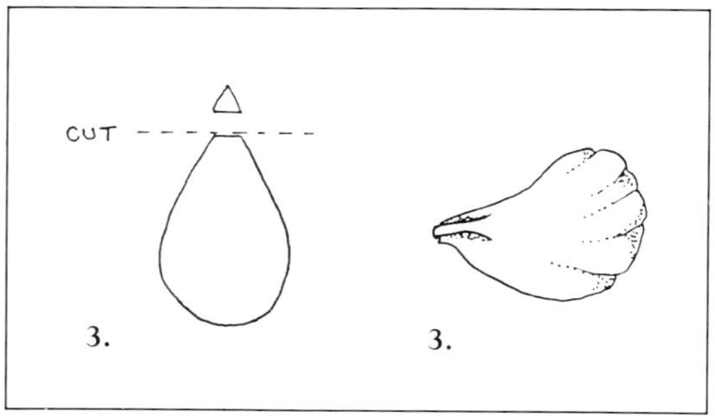

1. Using white flower paste, cut out five very small separate rose petals. Work on one petal at a time, keeping the others under a plastic cover to prevent drying out.

2. Thin and flute the top and side edges, and cup slightly.

3. Cut off the point of the lower end of the petal, but only the tiniest bit. This will allow the petal to sit closer to the stamens. Turn the petal over and mark a deep vein at the base with a tapestry needle for about 4mm (3/16th inch). This shows as a raised ridge on the right side.

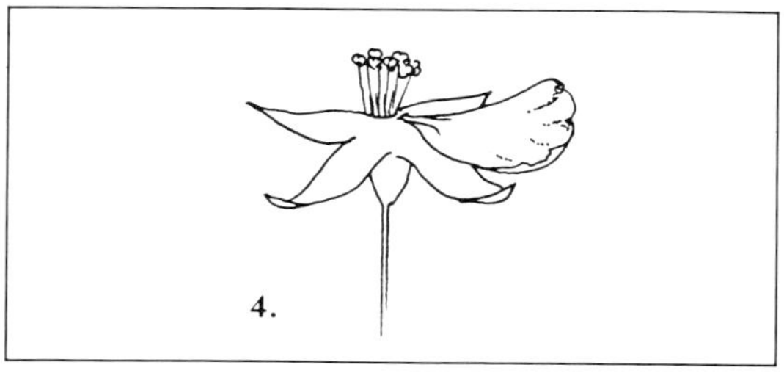

4. As each petal is ready, set it in place on the calyx: Brush egg white on to the calyx just at the base between two sepals and on the two adjacent edges of these two sepals. The petals have a tiny gap between each one, just allowing the sepals to show.

APPLE BLOSSOM

COLOURING

1. When the petals are completely dry, brush powder colour on to the back, on the left side only. Use a mixture of Sugar-Flair plum and fuchsia. Just tip the colour over the edge to the front.

Add a touch of green at at the base of each petal, and pink on the raised central vein.

TIGHTLY CLOSED BUDS

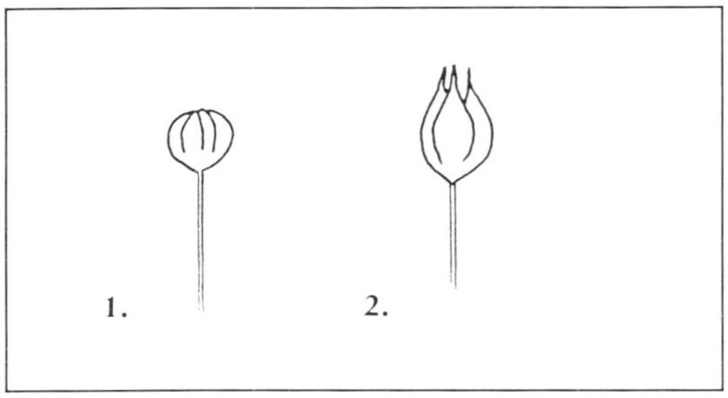

1. Roll a tiny ball of pink flower paste and push onto a 30 gauge green wire with a small hook. Mark five closed petals into the ball with a sharp blade. Leave to dry.

2. Cut out a very small calyx from apple green paste. Snip between each sepal then set in place over the petals, wrapping very tightly.

OPEN BUDS

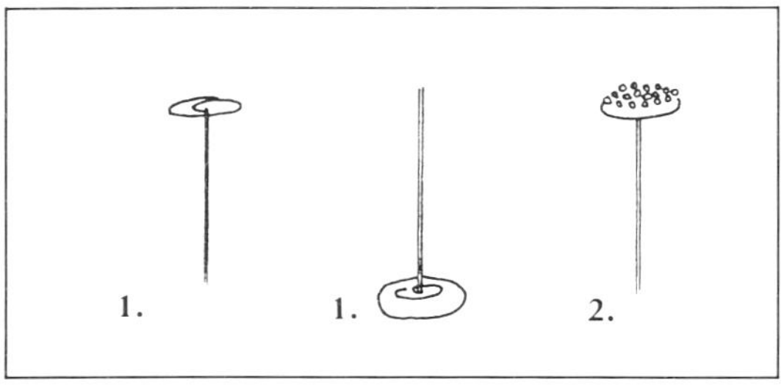

1. Make a small 'ski stick' on green 30g wire (see page 9). Roll a tiny ball of white paste, dip 'ski stick' into egg white and press into the ball until the paste 'oozes' through the wire.

2. Put a dab of egg white on the top only and dip into cream Sugar Tex (white with cream powder added). Leave to dry.

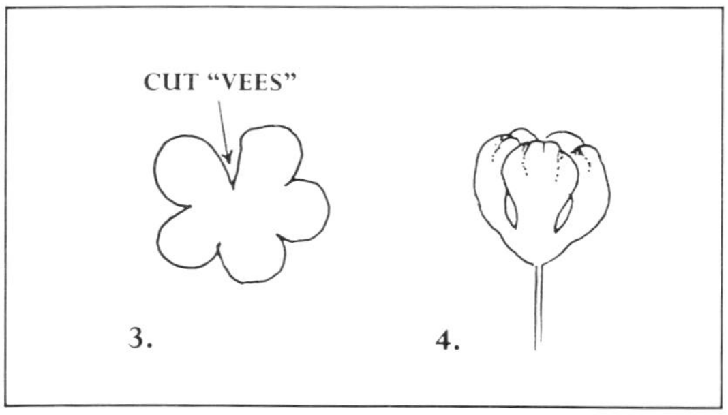

3. Cut out a medium sized blossom and cut out a small 'vee' between each petal. Thin, flute and cup.

4. Pull through the 'ski stick' centre and stick in place.

Dry with the petals curled up into a ball, or just slightly open, according to the stage of development required.

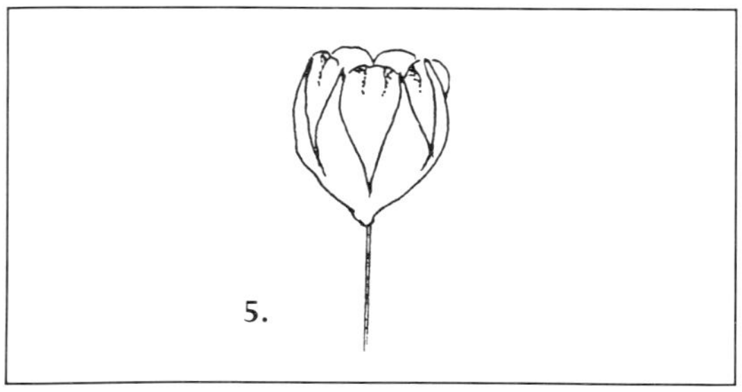

5. Cut out an apple green calyx. Thin and cup, then set in place around the petals.

6. Brush white powder over the back of all of the calices to make them look furry.

LEAVES

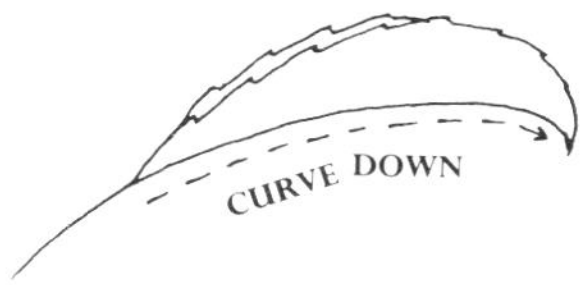

1. Colour flower paste apple green, and cut out leaves following the instructions on pages 10 and 11. The leaves are slightly toothed, so use a rose leaf cutter.

2. Brush shadow green on the lower half of the front of the leaves, but do not darken too much. Glaze with 'half glaze' and leave to dry for five minutes. As soon as you can handle the leaf, curve it back and fold up along the vein.

3. When the leaf is thoroughly dry, colour the veins on the back with a flat brush and shadow green.
NB: If you colour these veins before you glaze, you will probably lose the colour.

ASSEMBLY

Apple blossoms grow in 'crowns' of six flower heads, one in the centre and five round. The central flower opens first, with the 'crowns' at the lower end of the branch opening before those at the tip.

1. Tape six buds together to form the 'crown' at the tip of the branch. Use five tightly closed buds with one bud just beginning to open in the centre.

2. Begin to create the bark effect, using twig stem tape. Bind it tightly round and round the wires, twisting the tape as you go. Do this for about 2cms (¾ inch) only, then texture the bark by flicking and scratching with a strong needle or scribe, paying particular attention to disguising the overlaps of tape.

3. Tape in two small leaves, opposite each other, then continue to bind and texture the back as before up to the point where you want to add another 'crown' of buds and flowers.

4. Make up further 'crowns' as follows:
Five slightly open buds round one even more open bud. Five open buds round one fully open flower. Five fully open flowers round another fully open flower:

5. Copy a real apple branch or a good picture to complete the assembly of your branch. When it is finished, brush over the bark with opaque white paste colour with a little green added. This will make the bark look mildewed.

APPLE BLOSSOM

BLUEBELL

Spring never fails or falters
Come what may in any year
I will waken one fine morning
And the bluebells will be here.

Create your own breath of spring with this delightful flower. You need no cutters; just a pair of sharp scissors and nimble fingers.

BUDS

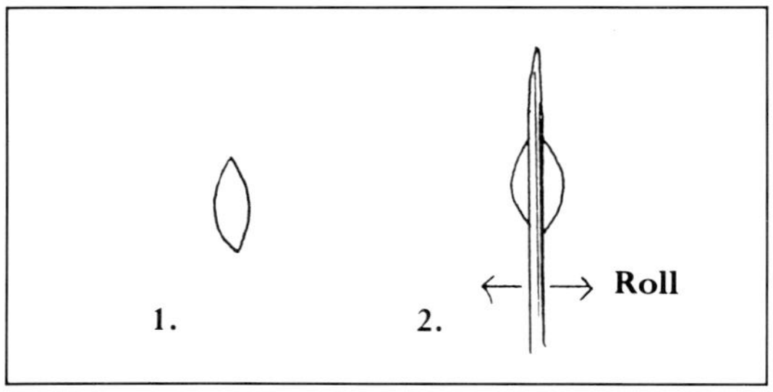

1. Colour flower paste a pretty mauvy blue. Not too dark, so that you can add a little extra colour to the finished flower.

Roll a very small ball of paste into a fat cigar.

2. Flatten and roll sideways with a cocktail stick.

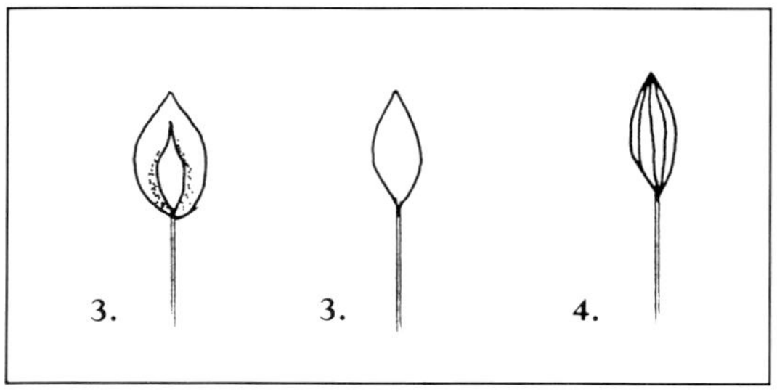

3. Moisten a large green 'onion' stamen, and press it firmly onto the paste. Wrap the paste around the stamen and roll into a slim cigar.

4. Mark bud with a sharp blade to resemble closed petals.

When dry, some of the buds may be brushed with moss green powder colour so that they appear to be less mature.

OPEN BUDS

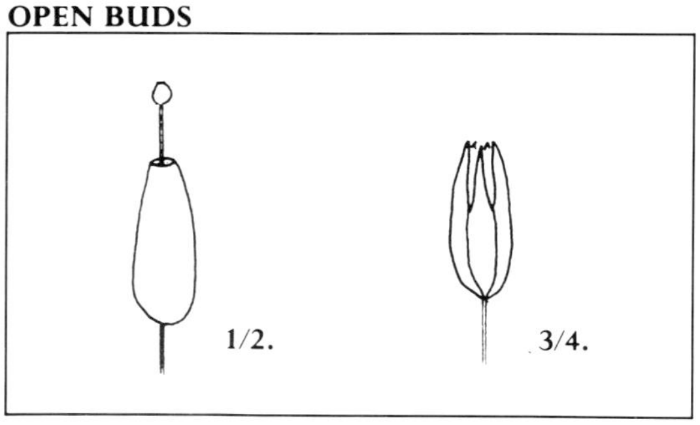

1. Make a small cone about $1\frac{1}{4}$ cms ($\frac{3}{5}^{ths}$ inch) long and open up the narrow end with a cocktail stick.

2. Pull through a green 'onion' stamen with its point cut off. Stick right down inside.

3. With fine sharp scissors, cut six slim and pointed petals and thin with the fingers.

4. Mark the cone with a blade as for the buds, between each petal.

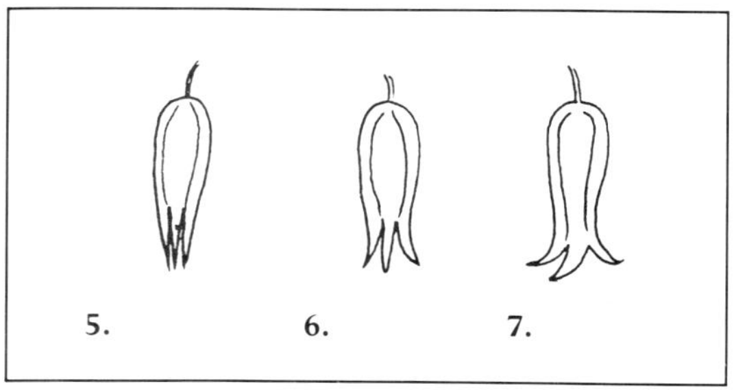

5. Close the petals until they appear to be just opening.

6. Make two or three more buds, but with the petals opening wider on each one.

7. Keeping the neck of the tube narrow, curl back the petals of most of the buds.

BLUEBELL

BLUEBELL

BRACTS

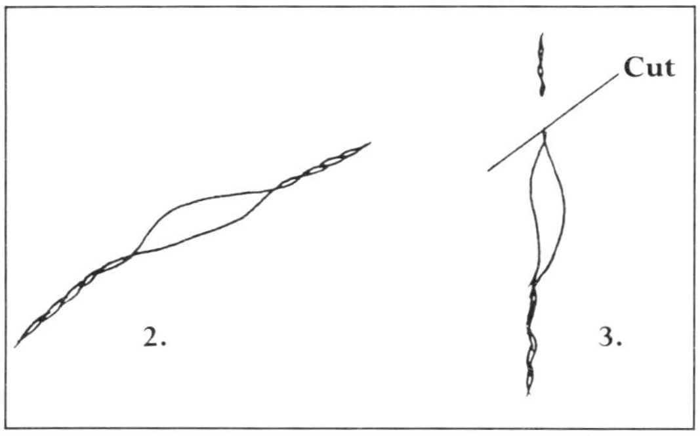

1. Colour a short length of green stem tape with cornflower blue powder, and cut with a tape shredder into quarter widths.

2. Twist one end of a short piece of tape very tightly. Leave 1 cm ($^{2}/_{5}{}^{ths}$ inch) untwisted, then twist again for another 2 cms ($^{3}/_{4}$ inch).

3. Cut off just above the untwisted part, making a point, as shown.

OPEN FLOWER

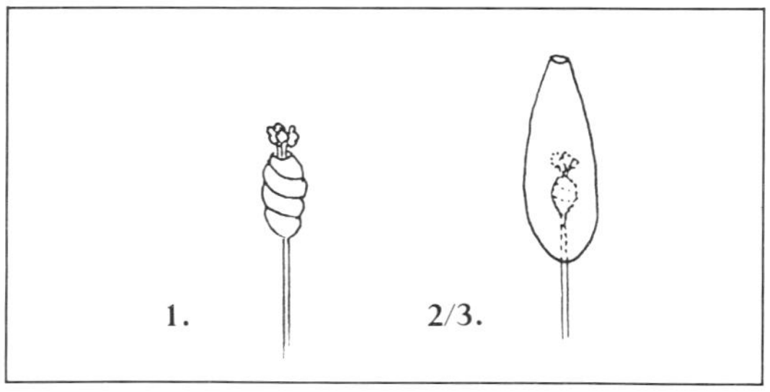

1. Tape four small yellow irregular stamens together, immediately behind their heads, with blue stem tape. Make a small fat 'pad' by taping round on the same spot. Cut off two of the stamen cottons close to the pad, and continue to tape down to the end.

2. With blue paste, roll a slim cone about 2 cms ($^{3}/_{4}$ inch) long. Open up the narrow end and hollow with the pointed end of a Honiton bobbin tool.

3. Pull through the stamens, using the pad of tape to secure into the flower.

4. Cut six long pointed petals. Thin each petal with the fingers and pull very carefully to lengthen them. Alternatively, you may prefer to roll the back of each petal on a board. Roll out towards the tip, then back again to curl.
The flower should be bell-shaped.
Leave to dry.

FLOWER ASSEMBLY

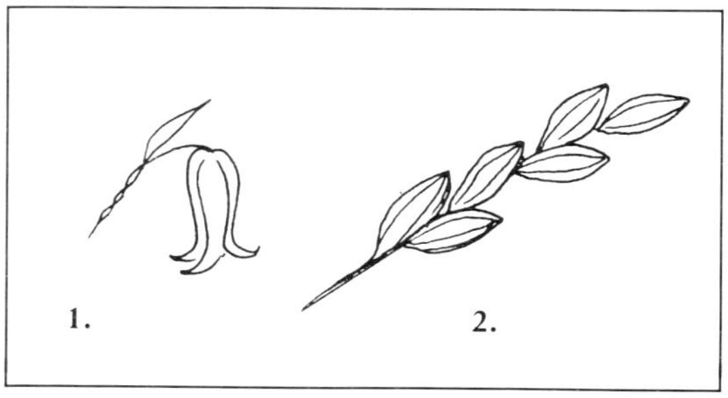

1. Using blue tape, attach a single bract to the stem of each open bud and to each flower. Leave only about 8 mm ($^{3}/_{10}{}^{ths}$ inch) between the flower and the bract.

2. Tape the six buds together, as shown, with very little space between them and no stalks showing. The greenest buds are at the tip.

3. Begin to add the open buds, with just a tiny space between them.
After the second open bud has been added, introduce a green 28 gauge wire.

4. Continue to add the open buds and then the flowers, one at a time, all falling to one side of the wire.

3 to 8.

5. As soon as the last flower has been added, introduce a green 24 gauge wire, and after taping down for about 2 cms (¾ inch), tape in another green 24 gauge wire.
Change to green tape and continue down to the end of the wire.

6. Disguise the change from blue to green tape by brushing over the join with blue powder.

7. Very carefully brush a little darker blue powder colour on the outside of the flowers.

8. Curve the flower stem over in a soft natural line.

LEAVES

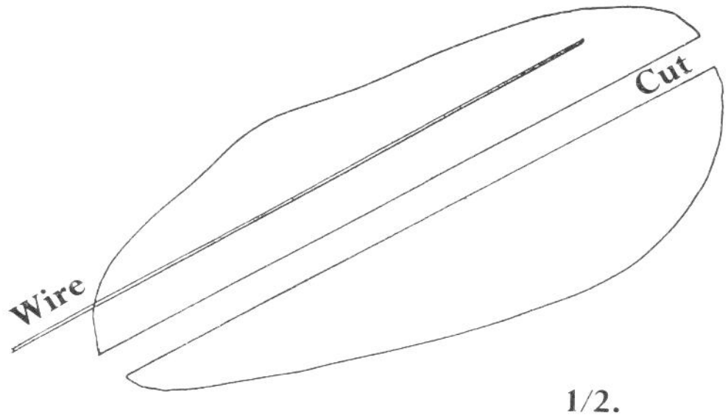

1/2.

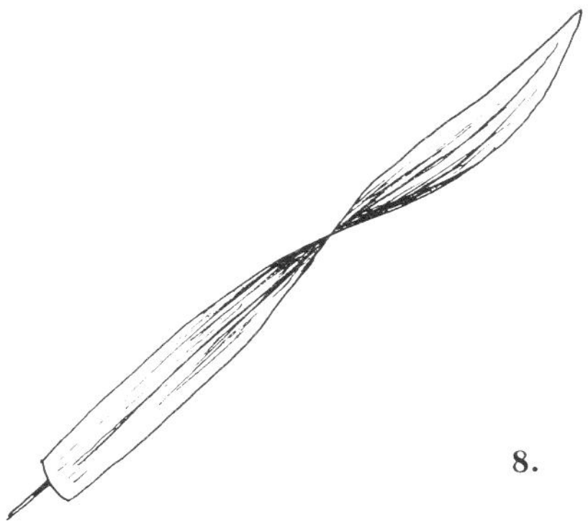

8.

Bluebell leaves are long and slim. They all grow from the base of the plant.

1. Colour flower paste a good fresh green. Roll out very thinly to about 18 cms x 7 cms (7 x 3 inches).

2. Dampen one half with a slightly moist 'J' cloth. Place a green 24 gauge wire down the centre, and cover with the other half.

3. Press firmly with the fingers, especially along the wire, and cut out an approximate leaf shape with a sharp knife.

4. Roll the edges of the leaf with a small rolling pin, until it is as fine as possible. Do not roll over the wire.

5. Cut out the leaf again, this time very accurately. Leave as little paste as possible beyond the tip of the wire, as this point is very vulnerable to breakage. Vein on a long veiner or corn cob.

6. Brush a little darker green powder colour up the centre, but don't lose the freshness.

7. Glaze with 'half glaze' by brushing on with a piece of rolled up kitchen towel. Blot and leave to dry for about ten minutes, by which time you should be able to handle the leaf.

8. Curve and twist the leaves as required.

PLANT ASSEMBLY

Hold all the flowers in one hand and adjust the stems to the various lengths required. Bind securely with fine silver wire. Add the leaves, one at a time, wiring as you go. Cover the wire with green stem tape right down to the end. Twist the wires round to form a 'stand' as described on page 9.

BOUGAINVILLEA

Remember any holiday and you will recall
How the Bougainvillea tumbled o'er the wall,
Pink and red and all the shades, how I love them all
Cascading down the balcony like a waterfall.

Although this shrub is native to the tropics, it can now be cultivated in this country. The individual blooms are set off by showy bracts with colours ranging from white and pale pink to orange, rust, bright red and purple. A taste of the summer holidays to come.

CLOSED BUDS

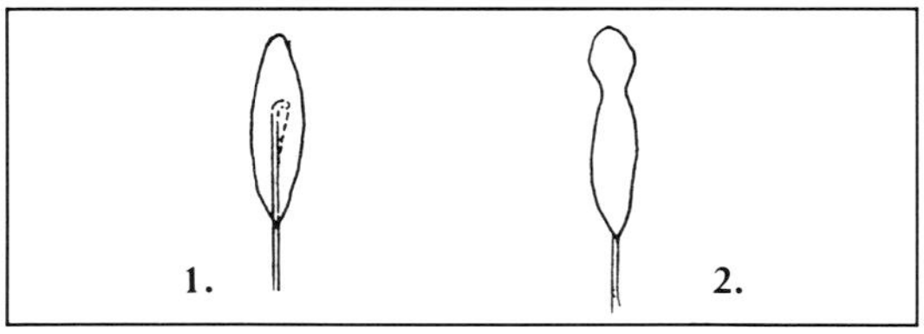

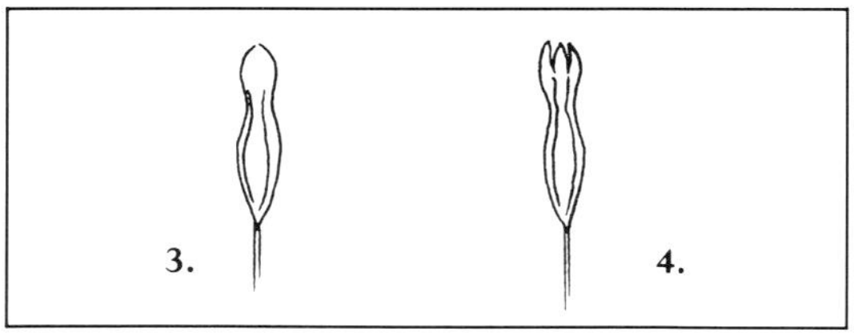

1. Make small closed hooks on 8 cm (3½ inch) pieces of 33 gauge white wire. Using white flower paste, roll a tiny cone about 1½ cms ($^{3/5}$ths inch). Make a small hole in the top with a slim sewing needle and insert the wire until the hook is well down inside.

2. Shape a narrow 'waist' close to the tip by rolling with the two forefingers.

3. Score five lines down the length of the cone with a sharp blade.

4. Make five tiny cuts in the tip with fine sharp scissors, for the closed petals. Do not thin or open these petals.

5. Leave to dry.

OPEN BUDS

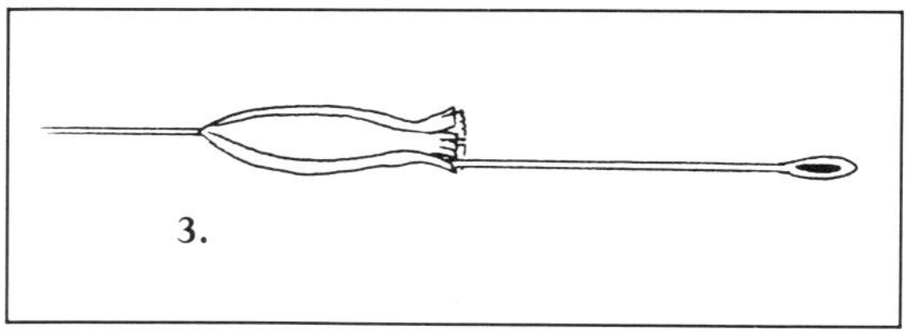

1. Make closed hooks as above. Roll small cones and 'waist' as before.

2. Insert a slim sewing needle into the tip, then using a size 13 tapestry needle, open up the throat. Pull through the hooked wire.

3. Cut five 'petals' with fine sharp scissors. With the slim sewing needle, press veins into each petal as many times as possible to create a tiny 'pleated' flower.

4. Push the petals up to make a bud with slightly open petals.

5. Score lines down the length of the cone as before.

6. Leave to dry.

OPEN FLOWER

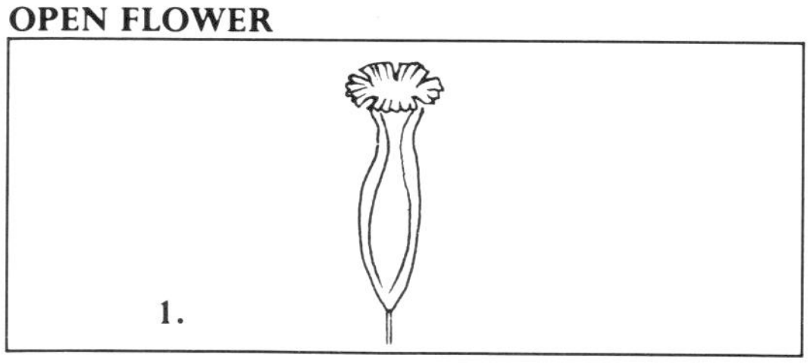

1. Repeat as for the open bud, but press the slim sewing needle into the petals a little more strongly to spread them into tiny 'fans'.

2. Leave to dry.

BOUGAINVILLEA

COLOURING

1. Brush all the buds and the flowers with Squire's Kitchen vine green powder colour, or a similar light, bright green. Then, using a flat brush and Sugar-Flair plum powder, draw the brush across the cuts on the cones, so that the colour is picked up on the ridges only.

2. Carry the colours up behind the flowers too, but do not colour the inside of the petals which should remain white.

BRACTS

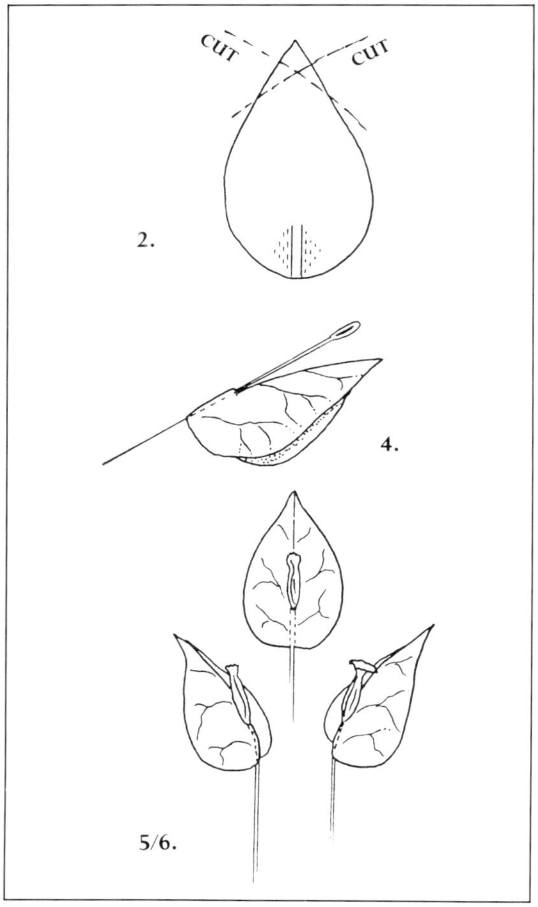

1. Use white flower paste or colour as required. Roll out paste *very* thinly, but make a short thicker vein at the lower end as shown.

2. Cut out the bract using a large rose petal cutter. If the shape is too pointed, trim away the point.

3. Vein well on both sides, using a good strong veiner such as an apple or young vibernum, but do not put any pressure on the thick vein.

4. Insert a fine needle into the vein as shown, bringing it out at the bottom.

5. Immediately pull through one of the bud wires until the lower tip of the bud fits into the hole made by the needle.

6. Fold the bract back giving it gentle movement. Pinch the vein at the front just a little so that the lower edges of the bracts stay back. This is very important otherwise the bracts won't sit close to each other when assembled.

7. Leave to dry before colouring.

COLOURING BRACTS

1. Brush powder colour onto the bracts with a flat brush working over the edges towards the bud or flower. Add the colour carefully but strongly. Do not allow grains of powder to get into the white flower. Leave the lower vein white.

2. Repeat colour on the back of the bract.

3. Brush a little vine green onto the lower vein.

4. Using a flat brush and vine green, brush colour across the veins on the back of the bract.

LEAVES

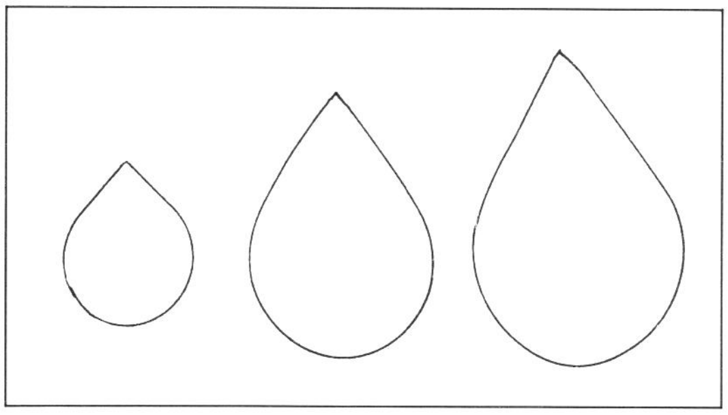

1. Colour flower paste Christmas green. Use a large rose petal cutter, and a veiner without too much detail as the leaves are fairly plain.

2. Follow the instructions on pages 10 and 11.

3. Brush a very little shadow green onto the leaves at the base, and an edging of vine green at the top.

4. Make several large and several medium leaves, and some quite small for the tip of the spray.

ASSEMBLY

1. Tape three bougainvillea bracts together as shown, using one closed bud, one open bud and one open flower in one group.

2. Continue taping three bracts together, but vary the centres.
Note: Newly open bracts have three closed buds, but as they mature, so there would be more open buds and more open flowers.

3. Tape two small leaves together for the tip of the spray. Tape down for a few centimeters then tape in two medium leaves opposite each other.

4. Add a bougainvillea with a short stalk, and continue taping in leaves and flowers as illustrated.

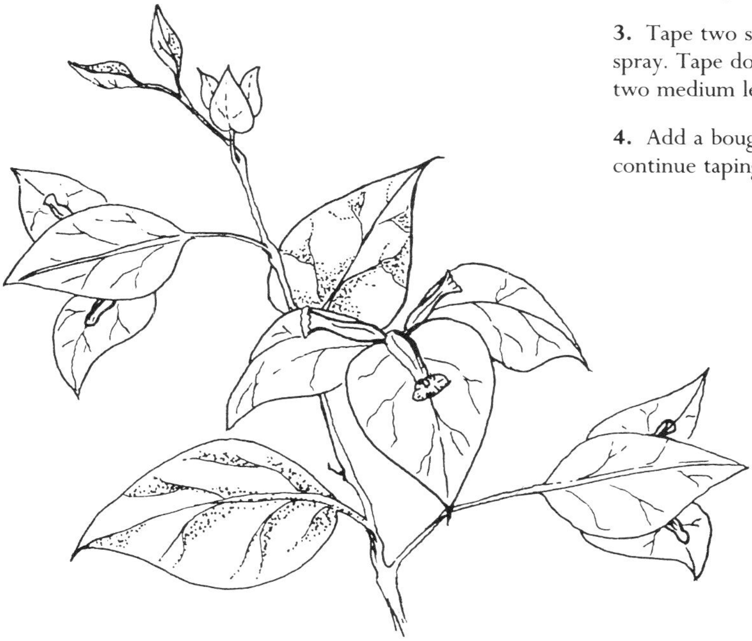

BOUGAINVILLEA

DAFFODIL

I wandered lonely as a cloud
That floats on high o'ver vales and hills,
When all at once I saw a crowd,
A host, of golden daffodils,
Beside the lake, beneath the trees,
Fluttering and dancing in the breeze.

Wordsworth may have cornered the market in poetic phrases about this beautiful flower, but he didn't know how to make it in sugar! This is your chance to prove that there is magic in the hands as well as in the written word.

PISTIL/STAMENS

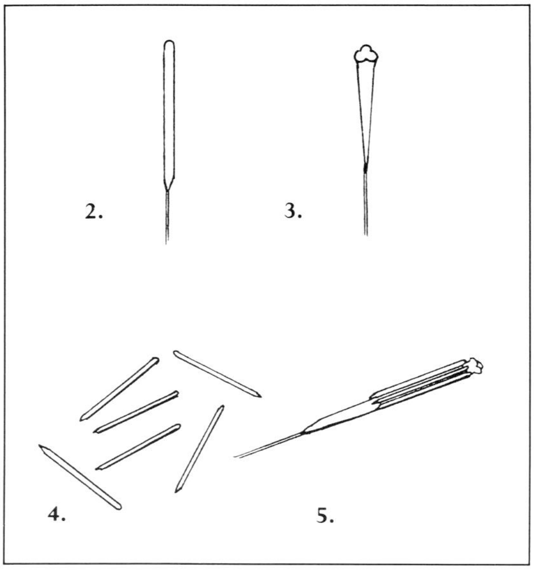

1. Colour flower paste the shade of yellow or orange required. Look at a garden seed catalogue to see the varieties available.

2. Take a very tiny ball of yellow paste and roll it into a slim sausage.
Insert a green 24 gauge wire, so that 2½ cms (1 inch) is covered by the paste, and the tip of the wire is within 2mm ($^{1}/_{10}{}^{th}$ inch) from the end.

3. Pinch three tiny lobes into the tip, for the stigma, not too pronounced.

4. Roll more yellow paste into very thin thread-like pieces, 1 mm ($^{1}/_{25}{}^{th}$ inch) in diameter. Cut into six 12 mm (½ inch) long bits, for the stamens.

5. Brush a thin coat of eggwhite onto the pistil, below the stigma, then press onto each stamen in turn so that they stick to the pistil as shown.
Adjust the spacing between the stamens.
Leave to dry thoroughly.

TRUMPET

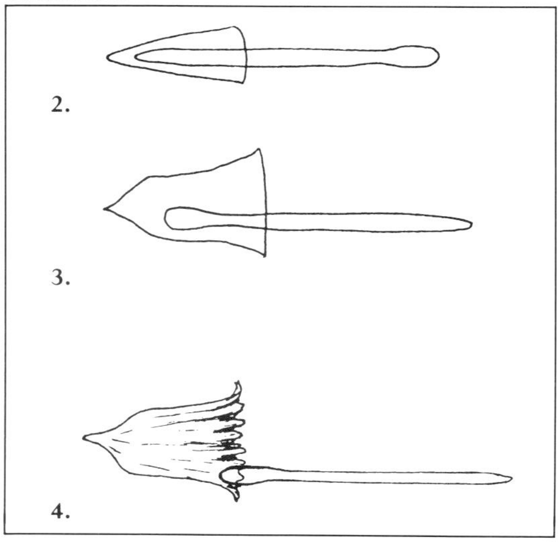

1. Take a small to medium pea-sized piece of flower paste and roll it into a cone about 2½ cms (1 inch) long.

2. Insert the pointed end of a Honiton bobbin or similar tool into the wide end and push it down almost to the tip. Keeping the point in place all the time, roll the cone on the board, gradually widening the throat.

3. Turn the tool round and using the broader end, roll the flower again about half way up inside the trumpet, to broaden the base.

4. Finally, thin and flute the extreme edge of the trumpet.

DAFFODIL/NARCISSUS

TRUMPET *cont.*

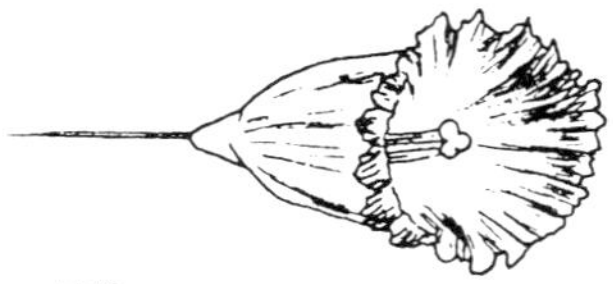

5/6.

5. Before curling the edges back, with the rolling tool still inside, press the trumpet onto a corn cob veiner to mark lines down its length.

6. Pull through the stamen/pistil centre until the lower half is in the base of the trumpet. Pinch this extension between the fingers to neaten and slim. This becomes the back of the flower to which the petals and sepals adhere.
Leave to dry thoroughly.

PETALS/SEPALS

1.

1. Using yellow paste, make a small Mexican hat with the slim 'crown' about $1\frac{1}{2}$ cms ($\frac{3}{5}^{ths}$ inch) long. Roll out the surrounding paste quite thinly and cut out the petals/sepals with Orchard six-petalled cutter N1 or N2 (according to the size of flower required).

2/3.

2. Thin and flute the six petals. If it is necessary lift the adjacent petals to the one you are working on, to allow room for it to be spread.
Note: Three of these become the petals and sit inside the other three which are now the sepals.

3. Vein all six petals/sepals on a corn cob veiner, or mark down the centre with a veining tool.

4/5.

4. Make a neat hole in the centre, pushing the tool into the 'crown' of the Mexican hat for the back of the trumpet to sit in.
Moisten and pull through to its position in the centre of the petals.

5. Slim the back of the flower and make a small 'hip' at the end of this stem, by shaping with a cocktail stick.

6. Dry with the petals in front of the sepals. Pinch the tips just a little and 'move' to soft natural shapes.

7. Brush bright green powder colour on to the 'hip' and very softly up the back of the flower towards the sepals.

STEM AND SPATHE

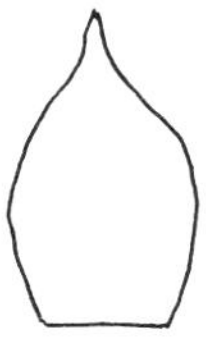

2.

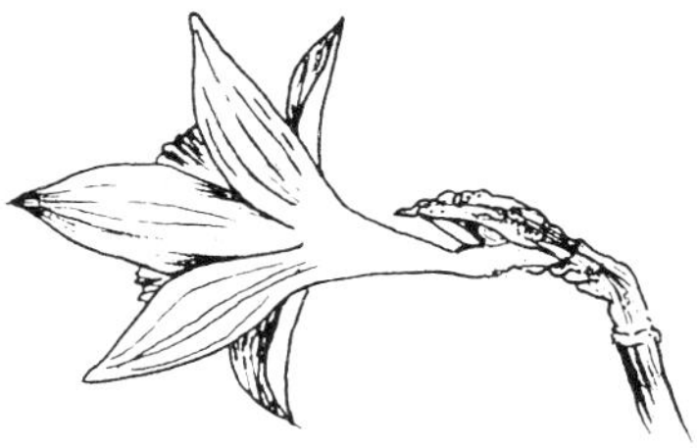

3.

1. Join in two more green 24 gauge wires, one on either side of the original wire, not on top. NB: The stem should be flattish rather than round. Tape right down.

2. Colour flower paste very light brown and roll out a small piece until absolutely paper thin. Cut out spathe using a template as shown.
Thin spathe and vein on a corn cob.

3. Wrap the straight edge of the spathe around the daffodil stem just below the green hip. Stick in place with the point either over or under the stem. Both are correct. Give the spathe a 'crumpled' look.

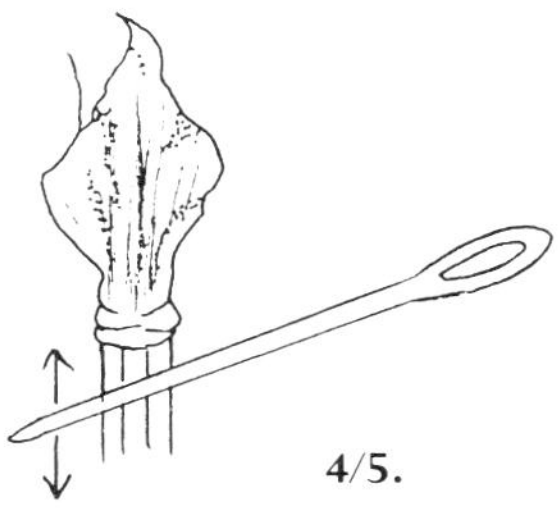

4/5.

4. Using green shiny plastic tape, bind over the join of the spathe and on down the stem.

5. 'Polish' the stem with a tapestry needle. This will eliminate the overlaps of the tape and give a smooth stem.

BUDS

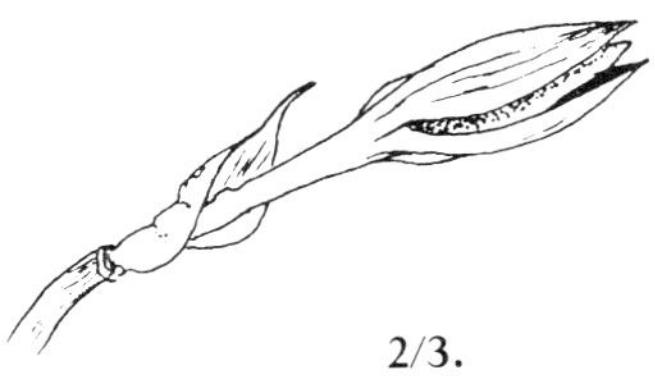

2/3.

1. Make a short, slim Mexican hat and cut out the six-petalled flower as before. Thin and vein the petals.

2. Pull through a hooked 24 gauge wire. Draw all the petals forward and wrap them around each other to form a soft 'tube'.

3. Slim the back of the bud, then finish as for the flower.

LEAVES

Follow the instructions for the Bluebell leaves on page 23.

When dry, the leaves may be brushed with a touch of white powder colour to give them a slight 'silvery' appearance.

ASSEMBLY

Hold all the flowers and buds in one hand and adjust the stems to the various lengths required. Bind securely with fine silver wire. Add the leaves, one at a time, wiring as you go. Cover the wire with green stem tape right down to the end. Twist the wires round to form a stand as described on page 9.

DAFFODIL

NARCISSUS

Narcissus gazed into a pool
Reflected there, the face he knew.
He fell and drowned, so says the tale,
And this enchanted flower grew.

Similar in construction to the golden Daffodil, yet the Narcissus or Jonquil has its own charm. Its cool, fresh colour is very complimentary when arranged with other spring flowers.

STAMENS

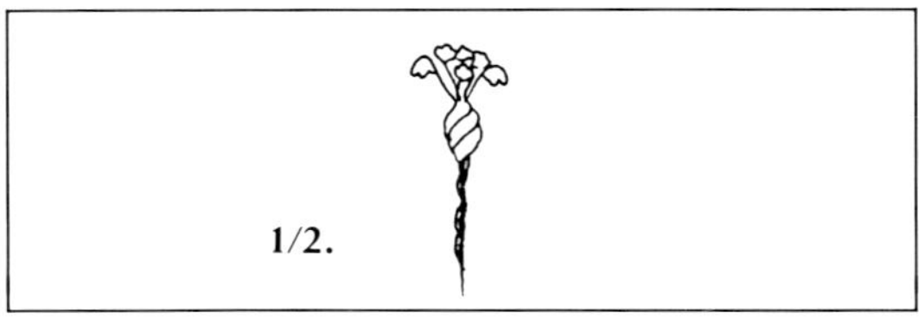

1. Colour the heads of small irregular stamens with egg yellow powder.
Using light green stem tape, attach six stamens to green 24 gauge wire, about 5 mm ($^1/_5{}^{th}$ inch) below their heads, forming a small pad with the tape.

2. Cut off the stamen cottons below the pad and continue taping down the wire for 3 cms (1¼ inches)

TRUMPET

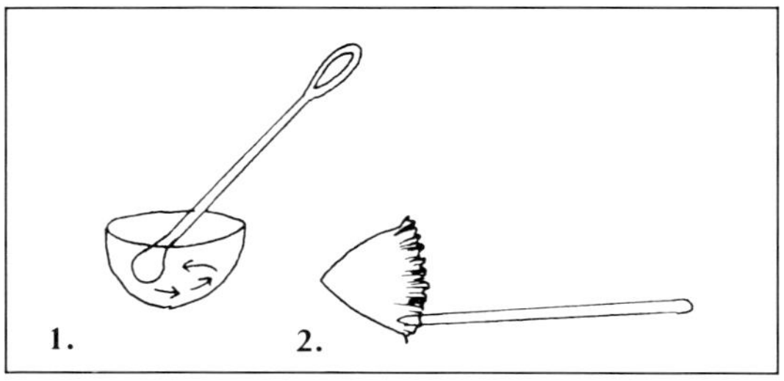

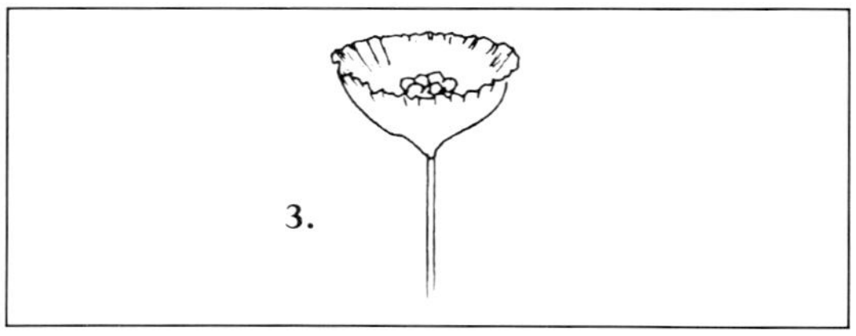

1. Take a very small ball of paste in the colour chosen for the flower centre. This may be white, yellow or orange.
Place the ball in the palm of the hand and begin to press in the centre with a very small ball tool.
NB: The Bodkin is ideal. Gradually circle round and round until a small hollow cup is formed. Judge the size very carefully. Don't make it too large.

2. Lay the trumpet on its side and frill the edges.

3. Pull through the stamens, pinching the back of the trumpet to ensure that it is well fixed to the wire.

PETALS/SEPALS

1. Using white paste, complete the flower as for the Daffodil.

2. Complete the back of the flower, the spathe and the stem as before.

3. When completely dry, tip the edges of the pale coloured trumpet with red or orange.

HAZEL CATKINS

In the music of the morning
Where the shadows meet and blend
The pollen chases sunbeams
As it hurries to descend.

There are several ways to make these delightful lambstails. The method given here is probably the most difficult and certainly the most time consuming, but there is no doubt at all that the results speak for themselves.

CATKIN

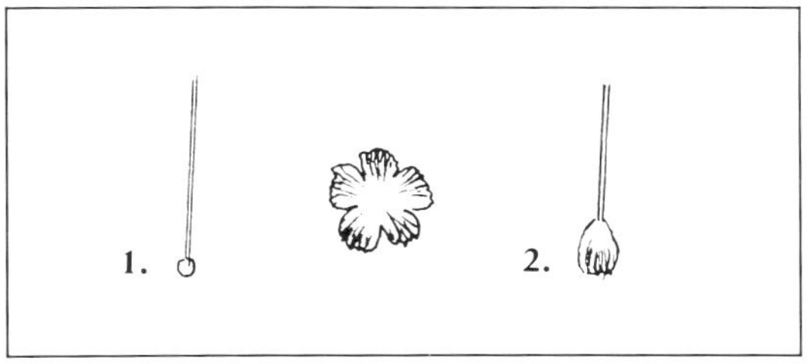

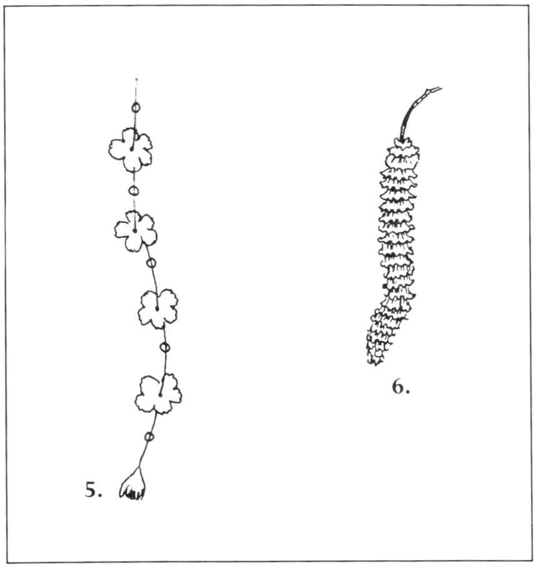

1. Colour flower paste light creamy yellow. Make a tiny hook on white 33 gauge wire and attach the tiniest 'dot' of paste possible.

2. Cut out a blossom, 6 mm (¼ inch) or less in diameter, from paste which has been rolled out until it is almost transparent.
Pull through the wire and draw the petals forward to hide the hook.

3. Roll a really tiny ball of paste, pass a fine sewing needle right through it, then thread onto the wire as a 'spacer'.

4. Cut out another fine blossom. Frill the edges as much as possible, then thread it on to the wire, and stick to the ball with a dab of moisture.

5. Continue to add 'spacers' and petals in this way until the catkin is about 1½ cms ($^3/_5$^{ths} inch) long, then curve the wire a little. NB: It is not possible to curve the wire when the catkin is finished because the petals are too fragile.

6. Continue until the catkin is 3½ to 4 cms (1½ inches) long.

7. Using a very soft brush, colour part of the catkin with light brown or pale green powder colour.

8. Tape the wire above the catkins with quarter-width olive green or twig stem tape.

NOTE:

There is an even more complicated way to make the catkin, without 'spacers'. You will need to roll out the paste a tiny bit thicker, then, leaving a tiny 'pimple' in the middle, roll out again so that the edges are very fine, and cut out the blossom. Frill the edges as before.

Press the tip of a cocktail stick into the 'pimple' to make a point. Pull through the wire and pinch the 'pimple' to hold it in place with a dab of moisture. The 'pimple' acts as the 'spacer'.

BUDS AND TWIG

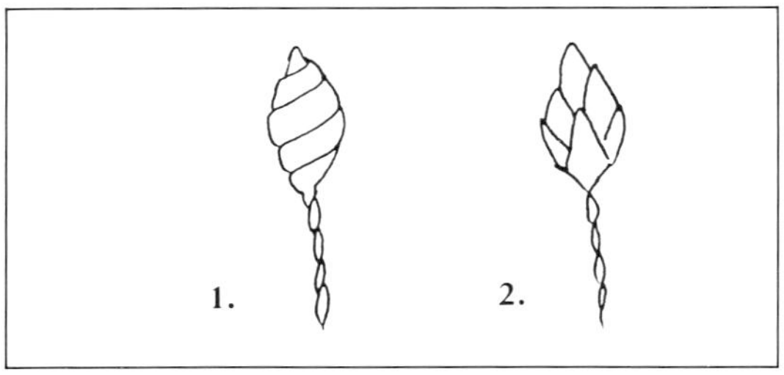

1. Attach quarter-width olive green or twig stem tape close to the tip of a half length 24 gauge wire. Bind around until a small pad has been made. Continue to bind above and below this pad to shape the bud as shown, then continue to tape down the wire for 1½ to 2 cms (¾ inch).

2. With very sharp, pointed scissors mark the scales, pinching rather than cutting with the blades. Prepare one of these buds for the tip of each twig.

FEMALE FLOWER

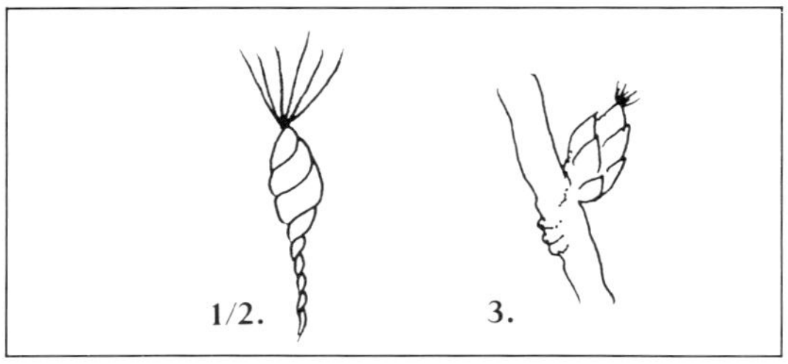

1. Cut six short lengths of cherry red Sylko and attach them to the tip of a short 33 gauge wire with olive green or twig stem tape.

2. Make a bud as before with the cottons growing out of the tip.

3. Trim the cottons to 2 mm ($^{1}/_{10}{}^{th}$ inch), then fluff them out with a needle.

Note: The female buds grow directly from the twig, without a stalk.

LEAVES (optional)

1. Colour flower paste a bright, fresh green. Follow the instructions on pages 10 and 11, using small plain leaf cutters and a hornbeam veiner (this is deeply veined just like a very young hazel leaf).

2. Brush the tips of the leaves with Vine green powder colour to make them look very tender.

ASSEMBLY

1. Tape one very small leaf just below one of the buds, then space the larger leaves, buds, female flower buds and catkins as shown.

2. Polish the twigs as you go, by rubbing them vigorously with a tapestry needle or the back of a pair of scissor blades.

Note that the catkins grow singly or in pairs. It would not be practical, considering the time involved in making them, to group three or more together.

HAZEL CATKINS

JAPANESE CHERRY BLOSSOM

Winter must change one day to Spring
Trees must blossom and birds must sing
Clouds turn silver that looked so black
All life's sunbeams be welcomed back.

The pink or white blossoms of this beautiful tree usually grow on bare twigs, but should the season be late, because of the frost, then leaves will appear amongst the flowers.

BUDS

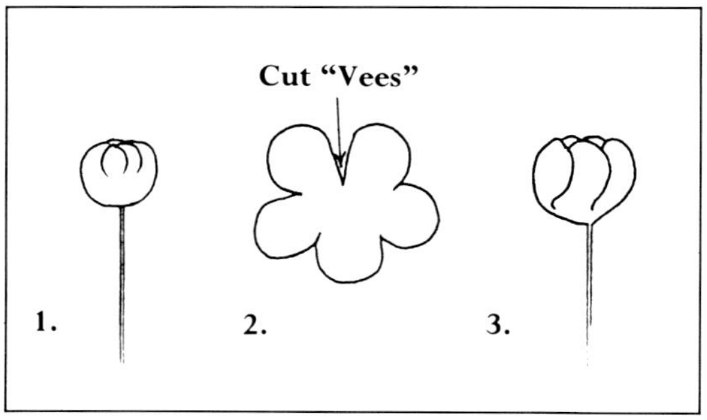

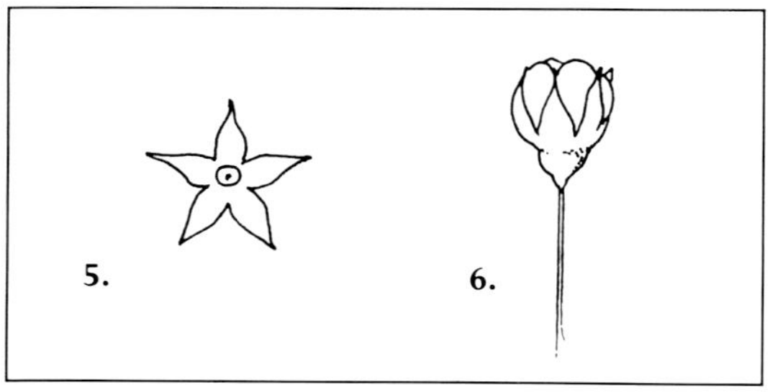

1. Colour flower paste pink, or leave white if preferred. Make tiny hooks on green 30 gauge wires. Roll a small ball of paste and insert the hook. Mark five unopened petals in the bud with a sharp blade. Leave to dry.

2. Cut out a very thin blossom, about 12 mm (½ inch) in diameter. Refine the edges and cup deeply, then snip between each petal to enable them to be overlapped.

3. Pull through the centre and stick in place with the petals tightly closed.

4. Tape the wire with quarter-width light green tape.

5. Using green paste, cut out the smallest calyx and thin if necessary but do not touch the points.

6. Place the calyx on a board and stick a tiny ball of green paste, about the size of a blackberry pip, in the centre. Immediately make a small hole right through the centre of the ball and the calyx with a fine sewing needle, then set in place below the bud, squeezing gently so that the ball makes a little 'hip' (inside the calyx).

OPEN BUD

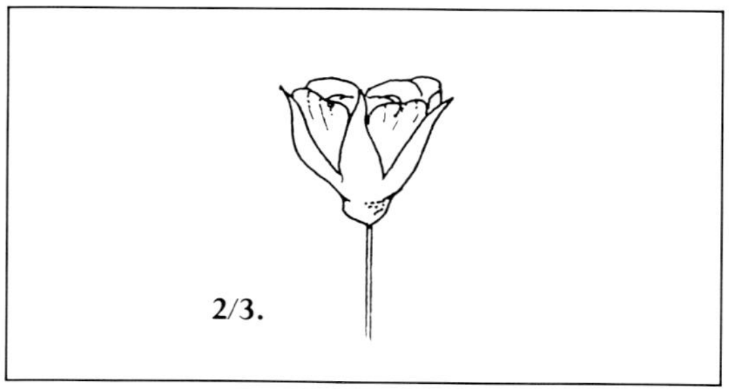

1. Follow steps 1 to 3 as for the closed bud.

2. Cut out another blossom the same size as before. Thin and cup and set in place around the first petals, but allow to open just a little.

3. Complete stem and calyx with hip as before.

JAPANESE CHERRY BLOSSOM

FLOWER

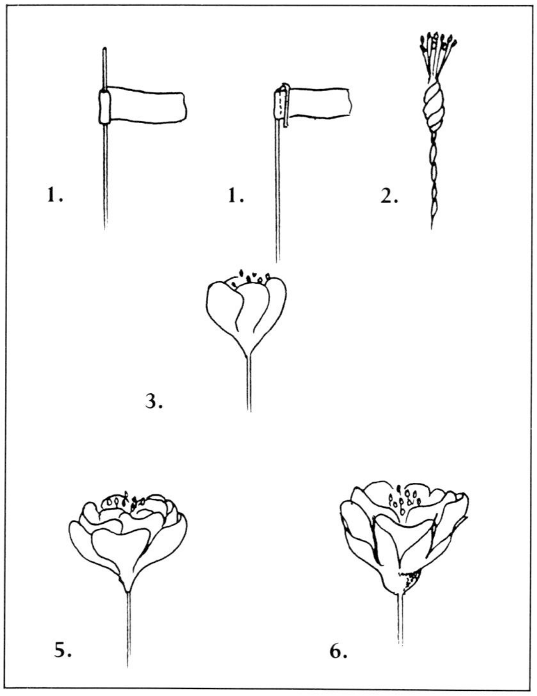

1. Prepare stamens: Join quarter-width light green tape to 30 gauge wire, about 6 mm (¼ inch) below the tip. Bend the tip of the wire down over the tape.

2. Tape in ten very small pink stamens, with their heads level about 1 cm ($^2/_5$ths inch) of the wire, making a small fat pad with the tape.

3. Cut off the stamen cottons immediately below the pad and continue to tape down the wire for about 3 cms (1¼ inches).

4. Cut out, thin and cup a 12 mm (½ inch) blossom and pull through the stamen centre until the pad of tape disappears, pinching the back of the flower to hold it on.

5. Cut out a blossom with an Orchard F10 cutter. Thin and slightly flute the petals and set in place behind the first petals.

6. Complete calyx and hip as before.

7. Make larger flowers by following 1 to 5 above, then add a second F10 blossom, so that there are now three rounds of petals.

LEAVES

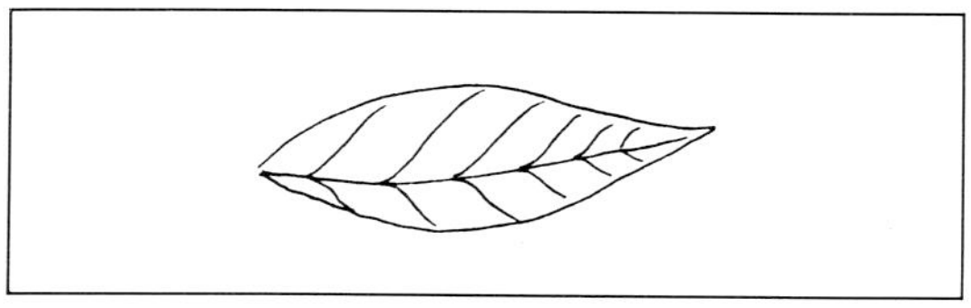

1. Colour flower paste light, fresh green. Follow instructions on pages 10 and 11, using a slim, long cutter and a veiner with parallel veins, such as a vibernum or very small cherry.

2. Brush some of the leaves, especially the very small ones, with pink or plum powder.

ASSEMBLY

JAPANESE CHERRY BLOSSOM

Cherry blossom grows in small clusters on long stalks (think of cherries). Use groups of closed and slightly open buds at the tip of the branch.

1. Tape several buds or flower stems together, or a mixture of both, with all the heads level, then add a small leaf with no stem showing.

2. Tape together two or three leaves with no stems.

3. Using dark brown tape, bind the flower or leaf groups to form a small knotty band by twisting tightly. Make this band about 5 mm (¼ inch) deep.

4. Continue to tape down the wire, keeping even thickness of the twig. Stop at the point where you intend to join in another group or branch.

5. Texture the knotty band by flicking and scratching with a strong needle or scribe.

6. Polish the rest of the twig by rubbing it vigorously with a tapestry needle or the back of a pair of scissor blades.

JAPONICA

If I could travel down those lanes
Where Spring begins and Winter wanes,
This is the path where I would find
Japonicas and joy entwined.

This beautiful shrub, also known as the dwarf quince, has waxy flowers in a variety of colours from white, through pink, coral, orange and crimson to brick red. These flowers together with tiny leaf shoots and long thorns combine to make an impressive arrangement with an oriental touch.

Colour paste cream, then add pink. This will give you a pretty coral shade. (Note that the buds and small flowers are made in the deepest shade, but add some white paste for the older and larger blooms).

CLOSED BUDS

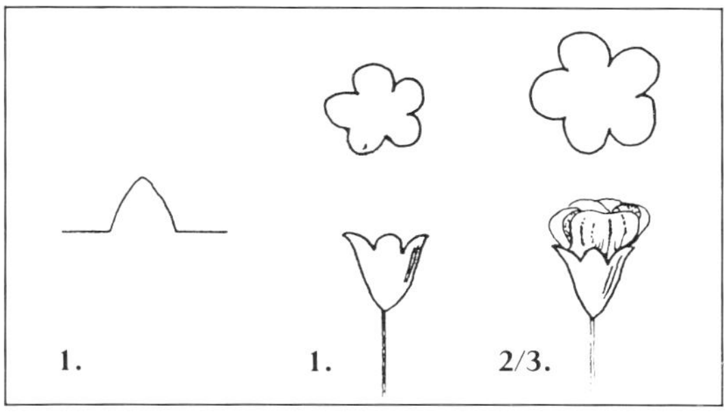

1. Using green paste, make a short fat Mexican hat, and cut out a medium blossom. Slightly indent the top, lifting the sepals upright. Place under a cup to prevent drying out.

2. Cut out a larger blossom in coral paste. Thin the edges and cup strongly to curl the petals into a ball.

3. Set the flower onto the calyx and immediately pull through a hooked green 30 gauge wire. Close the petals and leave to dry.

OPEN BUDS

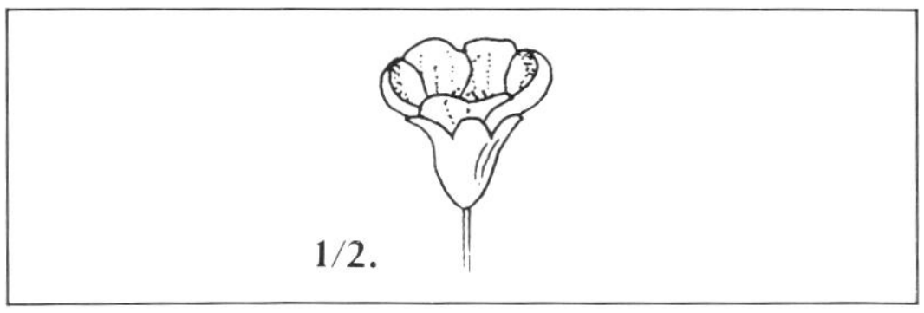

1. Follow the three steps as for the closed bud, but leave the petals slightly open.

2. Put a dot of egg white into the centre and sprinkle on a few grains of cream Sugar Tex (white sugar Tex with cream powder added).

FLOWER

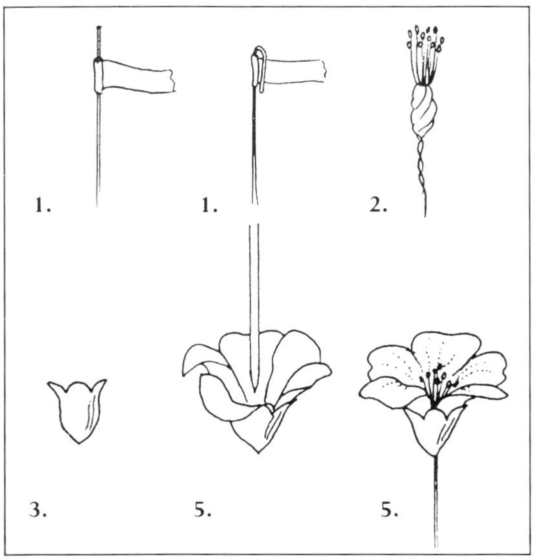

1. Prepare stamens: Join quarter-width twig stem tape to 30 gauge green wire, about 6 mm (¼ inch) below the tip. Bend the wire down over the tape.

2. Tape in ten very small yellow stamens, with their heads level about 7 mm ($\frac{3}{10}^{\text{ths}}$ inch) above the tip of the wire, making a small fat pad with the tape.

3. Make the calyx as before. Place under a cover to keep soft until the flower is ready.

4. Cut out the flower using a blossom cutter about 2 cms (¾ inch) in diameter. (Orchard blossom F9 and F10). Thin the edges and cup.

5. Set the petals in place on the calyx and make a small hole in the centre with a cocktail stick, then pull through the stamens until the pad of tape disappears down inside.

6. Brush the back of the palest flowers with a little pink powder. Add a touch of red to the calyx.

THORNS AND LEAF SHOOTS

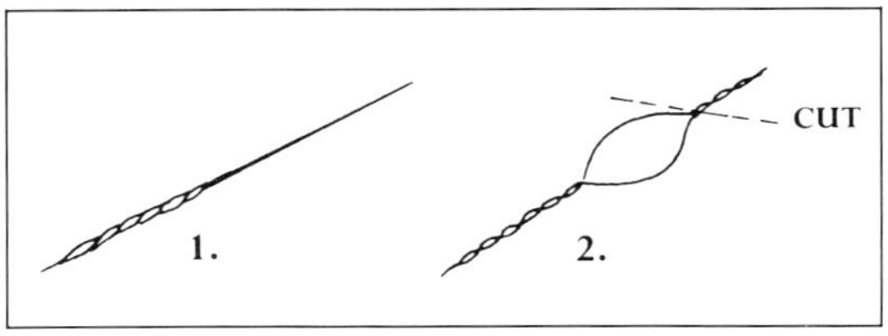

1. Make the thorns with quarter-width brown tape. Twist short lengths tightly and cut off to a point.

2. Make the leaf shoots with quarter-width bright green tape. Twist short lengths tightly, leave 1 cm ($^2/_5$ths inch) untwisted, then twist again down to the end. Cut off to a point.

LEAVES

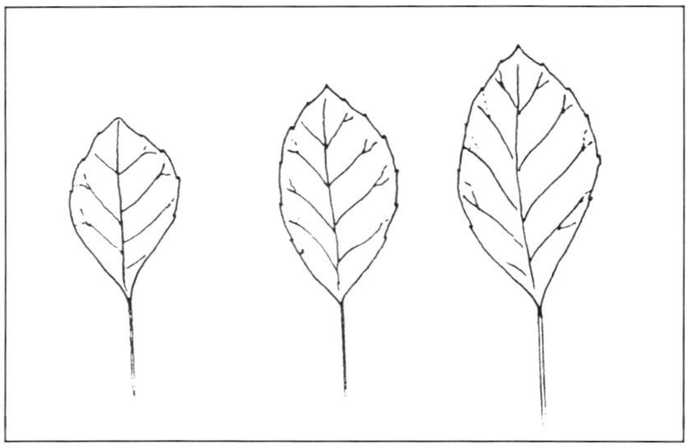

1. Japonica leaves are medium to long oval shape, with very small serrations. Use plain leaf cutters to follow the instructions on pages 10 and 11. Colour paste strong green.

2. Brush with a little shadow green to the front of the leaf, and a little red round the edge. The veining is not too pronounced. Use a vibernum or rose leaf veiner.

3. When the leaf has been glazed and left for five minutes, make a few indentations with a sharp blade round the fine edges.

ASSEMBLY

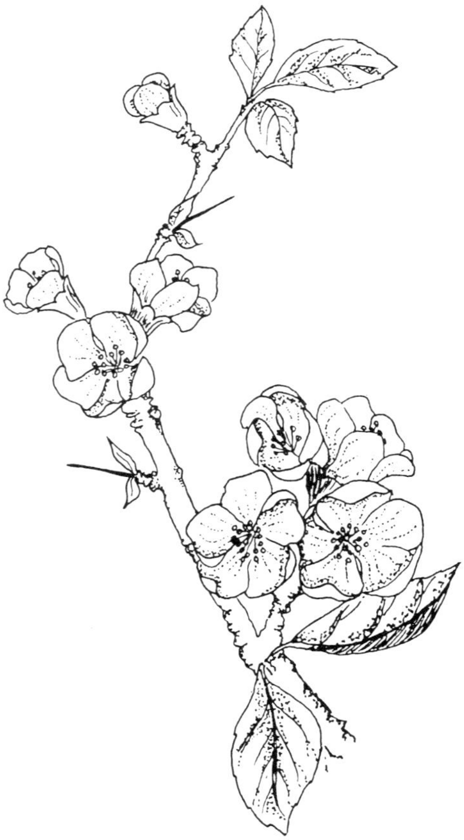

1. Join quarter-width twig stem tape behind each bud and flower and bind to thicken the wire for about 1 cm ($^2/_5$ths inch). Twist the tape as you go so that the surface is uneven, then roughen the tape with a strong sharp needle.

2. Tape together two or three leaves at the tip of each twig, then add a bud followed by a thorn and two leaf shoots.

3. Add more leaves, thorns and flowers as required, keeping the larger paler flowers for lower down the twig.

4. With a large needle or the back of a pair of scissor blades, 'polish' all the twigs until they are smooth.

JAPONICA

LILAC

I scarce believe in Springtime
Till I gaze upon that view
Of lilacs fragrant bowers
In my garden or at Kew.

"So real that you can almost smell it!" "Where on earth did you find lilac at this time of the year?" Just two of the comments that you may expect when you make this realistic spray.

There are many varieties of lilac in a range of beautiful colours, from white and cream, through pink, mauve and violet to deep magenta. Colour flower paste as required, using at least three shades of the same colour. Use the darkest shade for the buds and the lightest for the open flowers.

BUDS (make approx. 24)

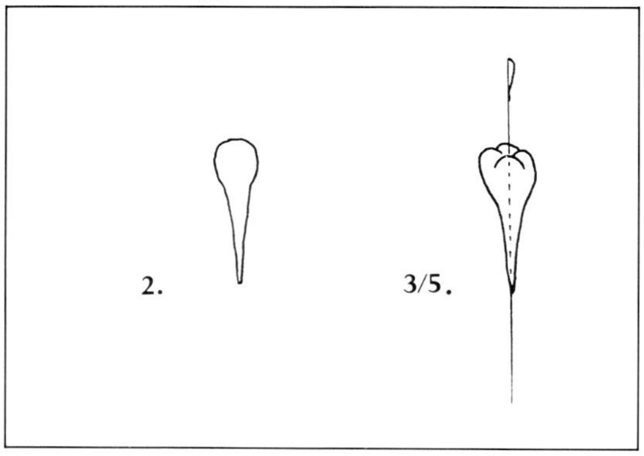

1. Cut 24 x 8 cm (3 inch) 30 gauge wires and make a tiny closed hook on each.

2. Roll a very small ball of paste in the palm of the hand, then elongate into a slim 'tadpole' shape, less than 1½ cms long (⅗ths inch).

3. Hold the 'head' between the thumb and forefinger and mark a deep cross with a sharp blade.

4. Pull the hooked wire through the centre of the cross until it disappears.

5. Gently roll the 'head' between the fingers to close the paste over the hook, then roll again just below the 'head' to emphasise the 'tadpole' shape.

6. Neaten the 'tail'.

OPEN BUDS (make approx. 24)

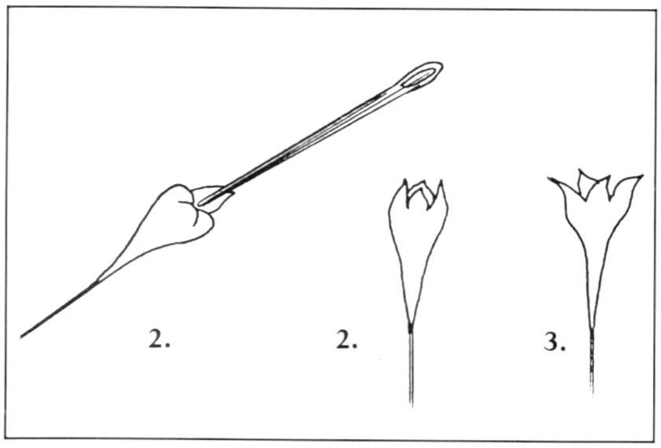

1. Follows steps 1 to 4 as for the bud.

2. Hold the bud by the wire just below the 'tail'. Rest the 'head' on the finger, then press the tip of a tapestry needle into the centre of the cross, against each quarter in turn, dragging out towards the tip. NOTE: The more pressure used, the more open will be the petals, thus open buds at varying stages of development can be made, from tight to almost fully open.

THE OPEN FLOWERS are made in two parts — a base cone, which is taped in with the buds and open buds, to form the 'skeleton' of the spray and the four-petalled flowers which are stuck on to the base cone when all the parts are in position. There are two reasons for this method. First, the flowers are very fragile and many will be broken if they are attached before assembly. Second, the flowers could be made by the Mexican hat method, but this would not allow the petals to be shaped with the tapestry needle with the amount of pressure needed to give the impression of a curled petal.

LILAC

OPEN FLOWER (make approx. 35)

Stage One: Flower Base

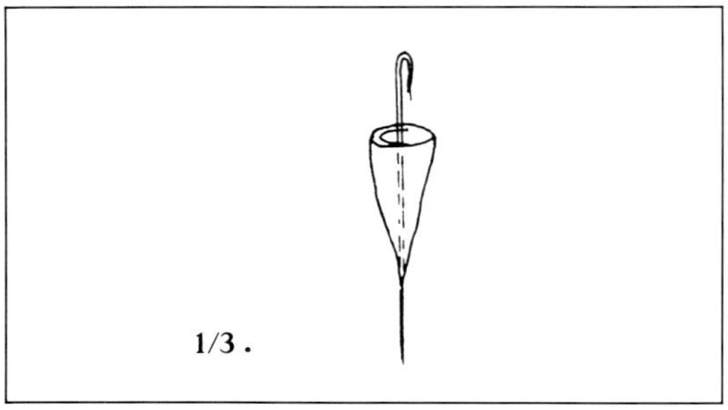

1. Make a tiny 'tadpole' as before, but instead of marking a cross, flatten the 'head' with the finger tip.

2. Indent a small hole in the top with the tip of the tapestry needle.

3. Pull through the hooked wire until it disappears (leave a small hollow in the 'head').

4. Neaten the 'tail' and leave to dry.

Stage Two: Flower Petals

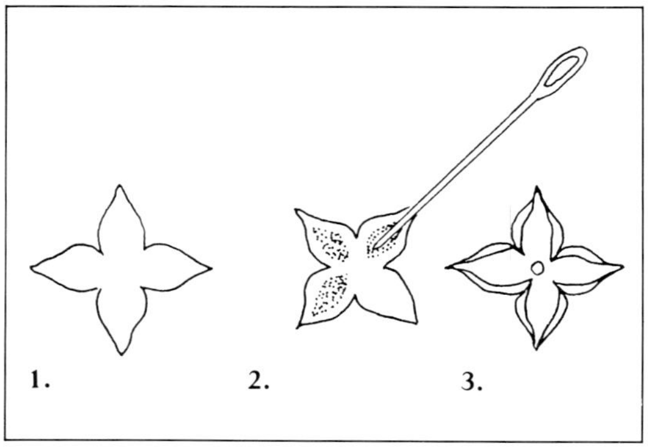

1. Roll out paste, not too thinly. Cut out one very small Daphne flower and place it on the palm of the hand.

2. With the tip of the tapestry needle press *very firmly* into the petal, not touching the centre of the flower. Drag out to the tip, using a 'scooping' movement, until there is barely any pressure as you reach the tip.
NOTE: It is the amount of pressure used here which creates the illusion of a curled petal.

3. Pass a sewing needle right through the centre of the flower to make a small neat hole, but before you remove the flower from the needle, pinch the tip of each petal very gently.
Leave to dry.

ASSEMBLY

1. Set out all the buds, open buds and flower base cones into groups of five or seven as shown on the chart.

2. Tape these groups together immediately below the 'tails'. Tape down for 3 cms (1¼ inches), cutting away all but two of the wires as you go.
NOTE: The buds and open buds must all be level, but the flower base cones are set a tiny bit lower, to allow for the flower to be fixed.

3. Introduce one 24 gauge wire to the top-most group. All other groups are attached to this wire.

4. Bend the wires of each group to about 1½ cms ($^{3}/_{5}$ths inch) below the 'tails' of the top groups, lengthening to 2 cms (¾ inch) on the middle groups and back to 1½ cms ($^{3}/_{5}$ths inch) on the lower groups.

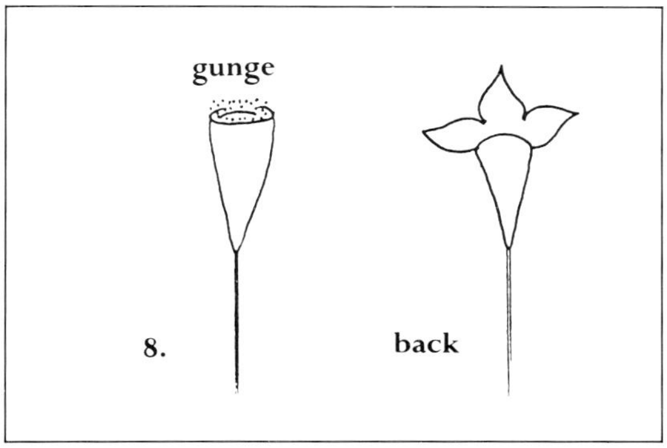

5. The groups marked 'x' on the chart form a small side shoot. Join these groups together on a 24-gauge wire, then attach this to the main stem below all but the final group.

6. Attach the final group very close to the stem to hide the join.

7. Move all the buds etc. into their own 'space' especially allowing room for the flowers to be attached to their base cones.

8. Finally, put a dot of 'gunge' (see Glossary) into the centre and round the rim of each flower base cone. Set the flowers in place, ensuring that they don't slip off before they are dry.

LEAVES

ASSEMBLY CHART

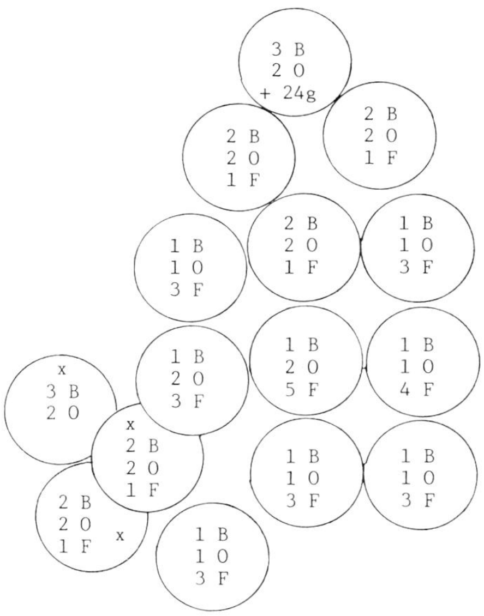

24 Buds (B)
24 Open buds (O)
32 Flowers (F)

1. Colour flower paste a light fresh green. Use large rose petal cutters and a veiner without too much detail. Lilac leaves are basically very plain. Follow the instructions on p. 10 and 11.

2. Brush on just a hint of shadow green at the base, and perhaps a touch of cream on the tips of a few leaves.

3. Attach leaves to a 24 gauge wire with light green tape. They grow opposite each other as illustrated.

4. Fix small sprays of leaves behind the flower sprays.

LILAC

LILY OF THE VALLEY

Brook no interruptions
In the sweet untroubled hours
And taste the morning fragrance
In the scent of lily flowers.

These beautiful flowers are very popular with brides for their wedding cake ornaments. They can be very time consuming to make, so here are three methods for you to try. I refer to them as being from the sublime to the ridiculous!

METHOD ONE (extremely quick and easy)

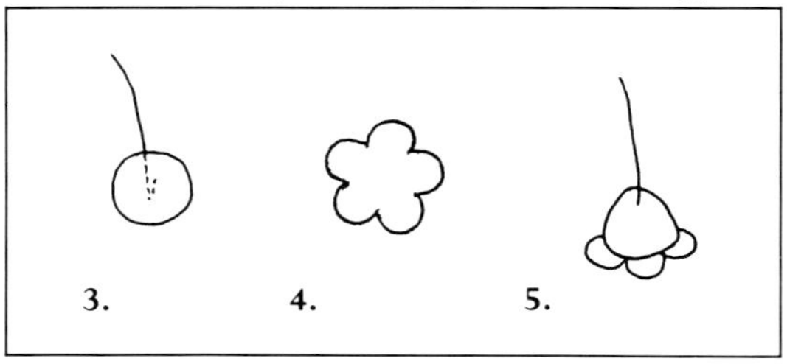

1. BUDS: Use large white stamens.

2. FLOWERS: Make very small hooks on cotton covered scientific wire (on a spool).

3. Roll a small ball of white paste and pull the hooked wire through until it is hidden.

4. Roll out white paste very thinly and cut out the smallest blossom. Thin the edges of the petals.

5. Stick the blossom to the base of the ball.

6. ASSEMBLY: As for method three.

METHOD TWO (not so quick but quite easy)

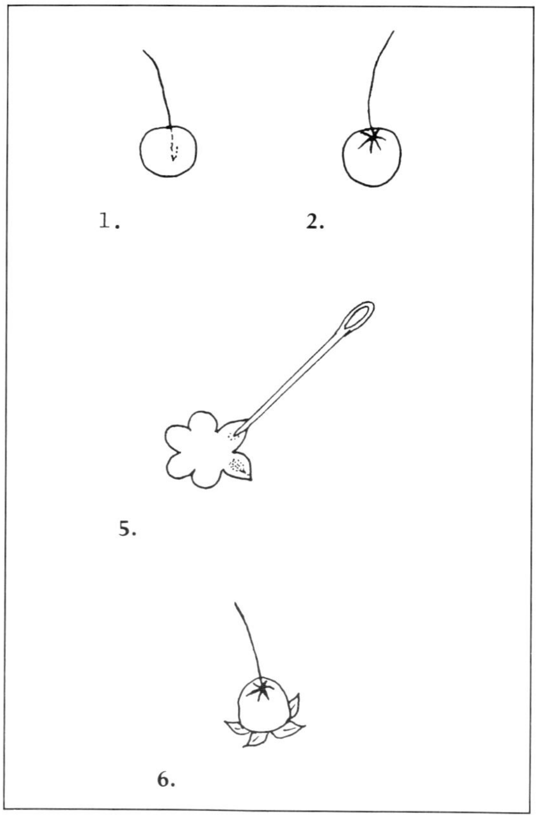

1. BUDS: Make a tiny hook on a short piece of scientific wire. Push into a very small ball of white paste, and shape into a neat round ball.

2. With a fine sewing needle, indent six small marks radiating out from the wire, as shown.
Make several buds in varying sizes.
Leave to dry.

3. Add some green paste colour to a few drops of water, and use this to colour the wire for about 2 cms (¾ inch) and let the colour run into the grooves on the bud.
Colour one or two of the smallest buds green all over.

4. FLOWERS: Follows steps 1 and 2 above, but make the balls larger.

5. Roll out white paste quite thinly, and cut out a blossom. Place this on the palm of the hand, and with the tip of a tapestry needle, press firmly into the tip of each petal, not touching the centre. Drag out to the point.

6. Stick the blossom to the base of the ball, then make a neat hole through the centre of the blossom and into the base of the ball. Curl the petals up at the tip.

7. Colour the wires and the grooves as above.

8. ASSEMBLY: As for method three.

LILY OF THE VALLEY

METHOD THREE (difficult)

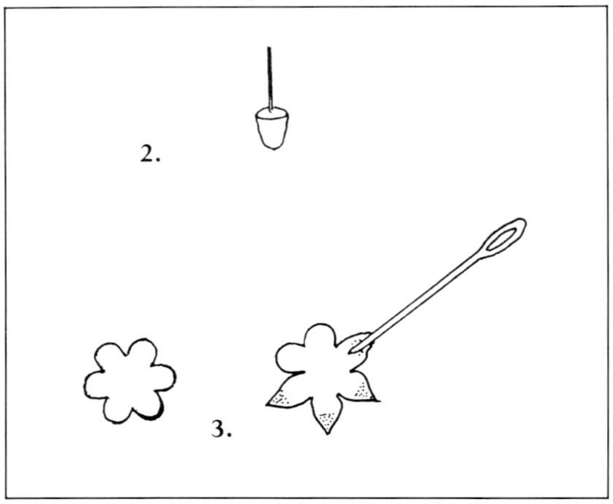

1. BUDS: Follow steps 1 to 3 as for method 2.

2. FLOWERS: Make a very small hook on scientific wire. Insert into a tiny ball of light green paste, making a flat top as shown. Colour the wire and leave to dry thoroughly.

3. Roll out white paste, not too thinly and cut out one flower, using the smallest blossom cutter or the miniature six-petal lily of the valley. Place flower on the palm of the hand, and with the tip of a tapestry needle, press firmly into the tip of each petal, not touching the centre of the flower. Drag out to the tip, keeping the flower as flat as possible.

4. Turn the flower over and repeat on the back of the petals (this will keep them flat whilst you shape the bell).

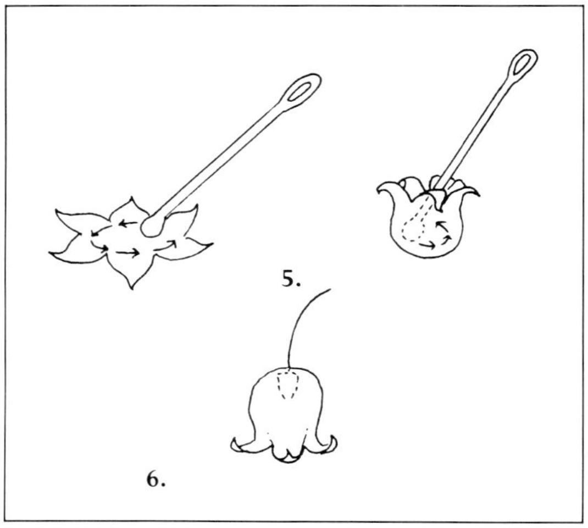

5. Place the flower on the palm of the hand again and using the ball tip of a bodkin, begin to make light circular movements round and round in the centre, beginning at the outer edge (not on the petals) and gradually working into the centre, creating a very fine bell).
NB: Only practise can tell you when to stop. Do not break through the paste.

6. Pull through the dry green centre and attach with water, used very sparingly.

ASSEMBLY (all methods)

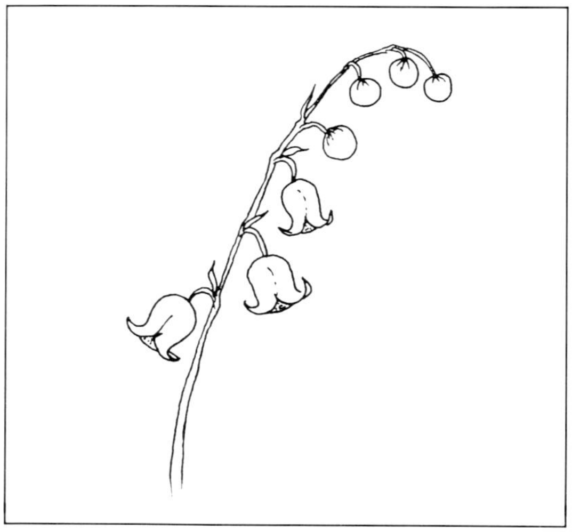

1. Use quarter-width light green stem tape and green 26 gauge wires.
Tape two stamens (method one) or the smallest bud to the top of the wire, then add further buds in size order, followed by the flowers, as shown.
Note that the stalks of the flowers are fractionally longer lower down the stem.

2. An optional extra for method 3 only, is to add a tiny light brown bract behind each flower. Simply cut a sliver of beige tape and tape it in.

LEAVES

1. Roll out light green paste thinly, to about 10 cms x 5 cms (4 inch x 2 inch). Cut in half lengthways.

Lay on a green 24 gauge wire down the middle of one half. Moisten the other half with a damp 'J' cloth and lay this on top of the first half.

2. Press along the wire centre to stick firmly. Roll out the two sides with a small rolling pin until fairly thin. Do not roll over the wire, or it will break through the paste.

3. Cut out the leaf, free hand, with a knife. Thin the edges with a ball tool. Vein on a corn cob veiner.

4. Brush a little Shadow green powder on the lower part of the leaf, and a little Vine green on the edges.

5. Glaze with 'half glaze' by brushing it on with a brush made of a small piece of rolled kitchen towel. Leave to dry for five minutes.

6. Twist, curl, and 'move' leaf as required.

LILY OF THE VALLEY

PERIWINKLE

Meadows wake in Springtime, hedgerows breathe a sigh,
Nature takes a brush to paint with colour from the sky.
Each tiny drop that mingles with a splash of morning dew
Leaves a star so perfect, a Periwinkle blue.

These dainty flowers with the striking contrast of their evergreen leaves, are perfect for a floral arrangement on a baby boy's Christening cake, or with primroses for Easter.

FLOWER

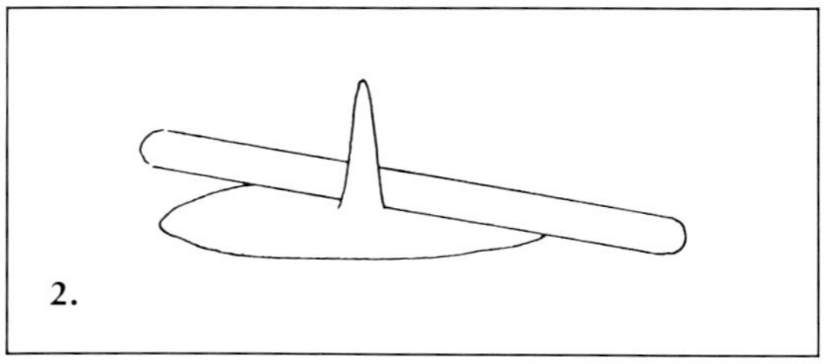

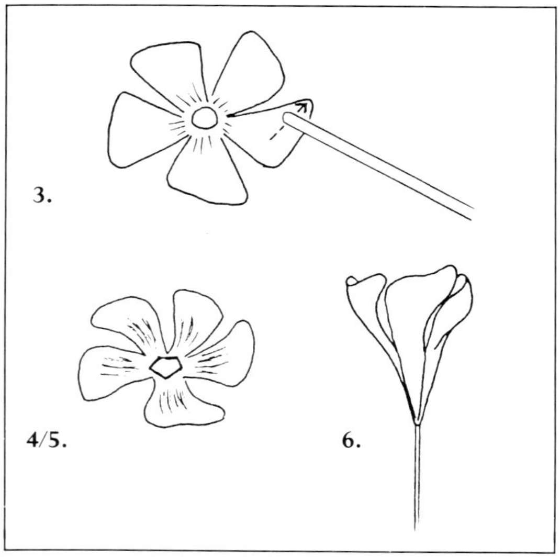

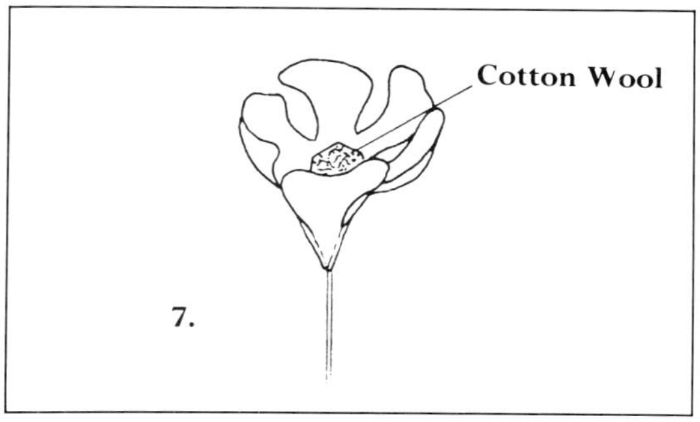

1. Mix Sugarflair powder colours: Cornflower Blue and Fuchsia, until a mauvy blue is obtained.
Cover half-length green 26 gauge wires with quarter-width light green tape.
Make a small hook on each.

2. Use white paste, so that the petals may be coloured blue whilst leaving the centre white.
Roll out paste with a small, very slim Mexican hat, with the 'crown' about 1 cm ($\frac{2}{5}$ths inch) long. Thin the paste all round, especially close to the base of the 'crown'.

3. Cut out the flower using a small periwinkle, phlox or dianthus cutter.
With the flower flat on the board, roll each petal until very fine and slightly spread. Give an extra little roll on the right hand corner as shown, to stretch the tip. Do not overdo this.

4. Hold the 'crown' between the fingers, soften and slightly cup the front of the petals with a small ball tool.

5. Indent into the centre with a small five-sided veining tool. If this is not available, use the tip of a Honiton bobbin or cocktail stick. Pull through the taped, hooked wire until the tip disappears well down inside, leaving the throat open.

6. Indent five veins into the back of the flower base with a blade. Each vein is in between the petals. Leave to dry thoroughly. This is important.

7. Push a small piece of cotton wool right down inside the throat to protect it from the powder colour. Brush the blue/fuchsia powder on each petal, working from the edge down to the centre. Work carefully and patiently until you achieve a really good shaded effect with the edges slightly darker than the centre.

PERIWINKLE

FLOWER *cont.*

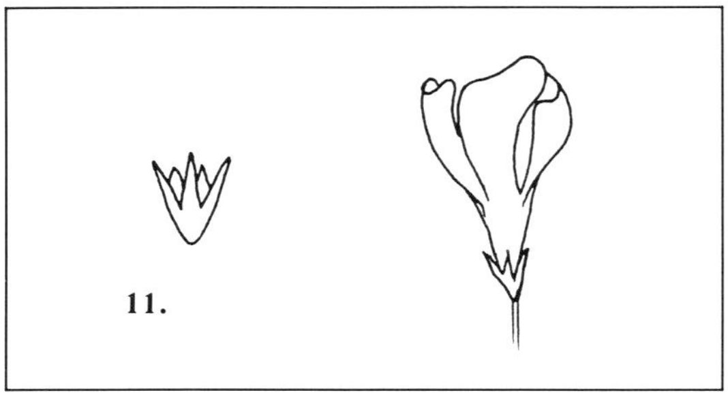

8. Using a tiny brush, insert a little vine green powder colour right down inside the throat.

9. Colour the back of the petals and the ridges on the back of the flower, with blue, then put a streak of vine green up the five indentations.

10. Drop a ball of white paste, about the size of a pinhead, into the throat. Push it well down inside, then add a dab of vine green.

11. The calyx is made with a tiny ball of white paste. Roll into a cone and cut five pointed sepals. Stick to the base of the flower as shown. Brush with vine green.

BUDS

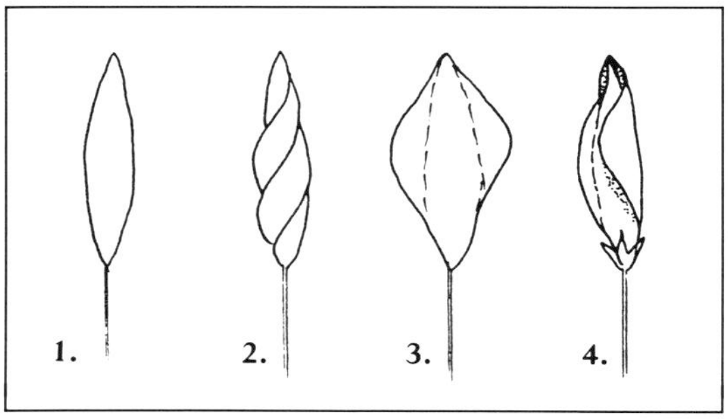

1. Prepare wires as for the flower. Roll a small ball of white flower paste into a slim cone. Insert the hooked wire.

2. Mark several closed petals down its length with a sharp blade and give the cone a twist to spiral the petals round.

3. Alternatively, the petals may be pinched out from the cone and wrapped round. Buds of varying stages may be made using both of these methods.

4. Colour the bud with blue/fuchsia powder as before, with a touch of vine green at the base. Make the calyx as for the flower.

LEAVES

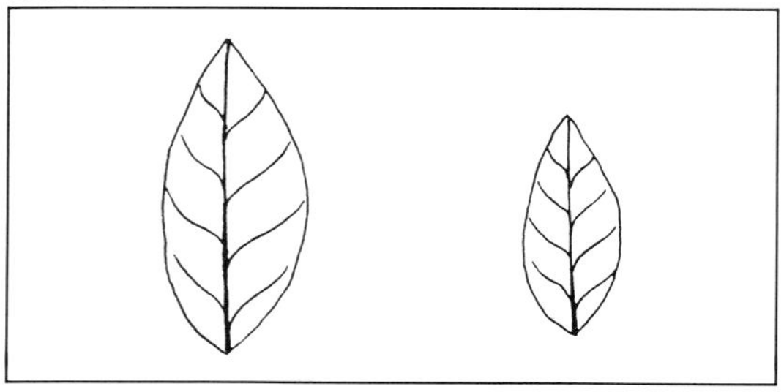

1. Make leaves as shown on pages 10 and 11. Use a plain oval cutter in several sizes from 1 to 4 cms (½ inch to 1½ inch). The veining is very simple.

2. Colour base a good strong green, then brush on shadow green over the front of the leaf, trying to avoid colouring the centre vein.

ASSEMBLY

1. Attach two tiny leaves to the top of a green 26 gauge wire. Tape down for about 2 cms (¾ inch) then tape in two slightly larger leaves.

2. Continue adding leaves in pairs, with a flower on a short stem, or a bud as shown.

3. Periwinkle sprays may be set into a paste base or trailing over the cake as required.

PERIWINKLE

PRIMROSE

Stamen by stamen and leaf by leaf
The earth grows lovely beyond belief
Primrose by primrose the air grows sweet
Mixing and making the spring complete.

The delicate, softly coloured primrose is surely the most welcome herald of spring. A small arrangement of flowers with their distinctive leaves makes a lovely centre piece.

CALYX

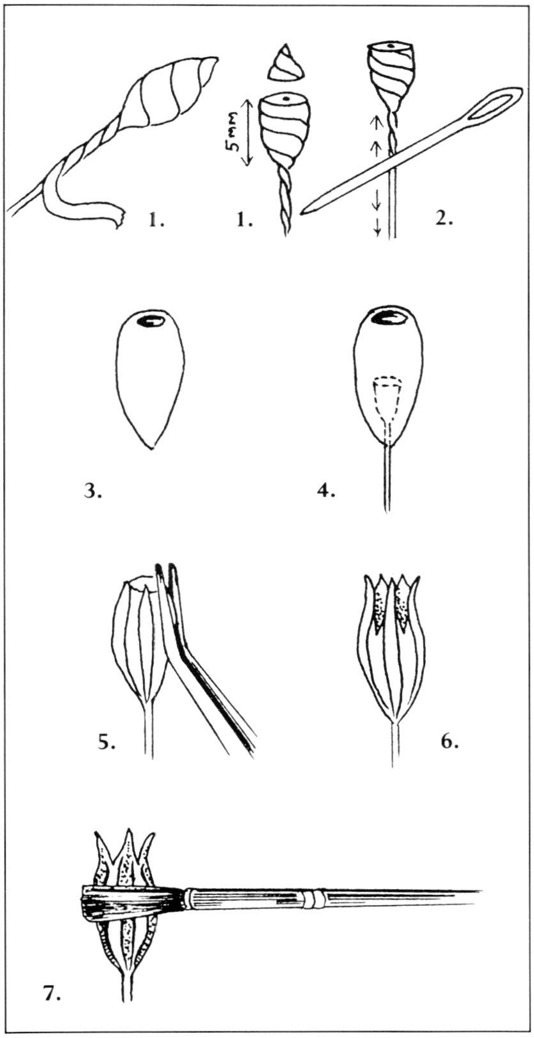

1. Cover an 18 cm (7 inch) 24 gauge white wire with half-width white tape, making a neat pad of tape at the top. Cut off the tip of this pad, leaving about 5 mm ($\frac{1}{5}$th inch.

2. 'Polish' the stem with a tapestry needle. This will eliminate the overlaps of the tape and give a smooth stem.

3. Colour flower paste pale yellow. Roll a small ball into a cone about 1½ cms ($\frac{3}{5}$ths inch) long. Pass a slim sewing needle right through, then widen the top of the hole with the tip of the tapestry needle.

4. Moisten the pad and pull the stem through the cone until the pad disappears deep down inside.

5. Using cranked tweezers, carefully pinch five ridges down the length of the cone, starting at the top and narrowing at the base. If necessary indent between the ridges to improve the shape.

6. Using very slim sharp scissors, snip out a narrow 'vee' between each ridge as shown.

7. Brush the stem and the calyx with a light fresh green powder colour, then, using a flat brush and rose pink powder colour, brush across the ridges at right angles, so that the colour is only picked up on the ridges and nowhere else. Also brush a little pink on the stem. Leave to dry.

TIP

Careful use of powder colour is extremely important. Use a piece of kitchen towel, taking the colour from the pot to the paper and working the colour well into the brush until there are no loose grains. In this way you will have complete control over the colour you are using. It is much easier to add more colour than to remove any excess.

PETALS

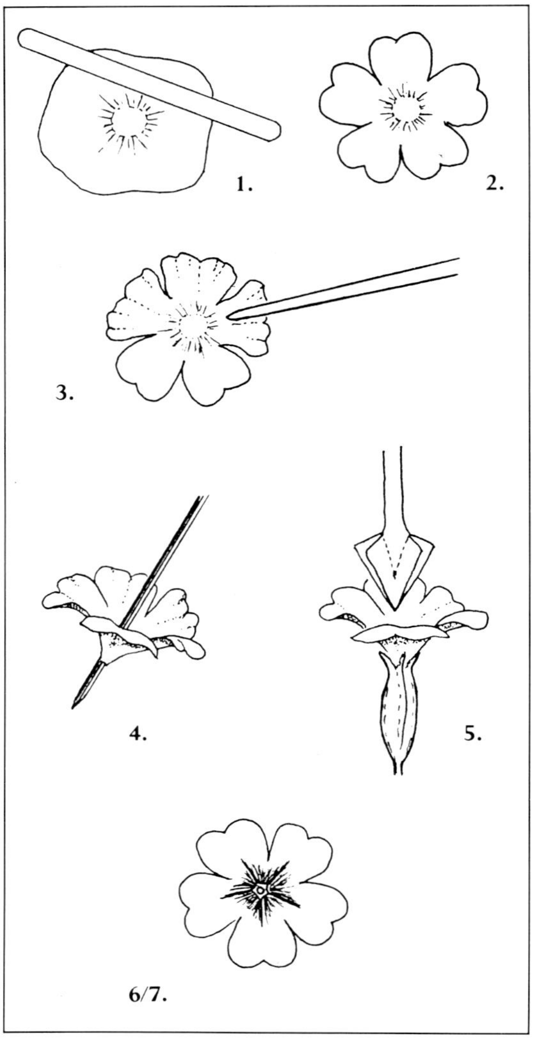

1. Roll out a small piece of pale yellow paste, not too thinly. Continue to roll round the edges, leaving a tiny 'pimple' of thicker paste in the centre, about 5 mm ($^1/_5{}^{th}$ inch) in diameter.

2. Cut out a medium primrose flower, making sure that the 'pimple' is right in the centre.

3. Using a very small rolling tool, thin each of the petals by rolling from the side to the centre on each half of the heart shape, paying particular attention to the edges.

4. Push the point of a cocktail stick into the centre of the 'pimple' and, at the same time, pinch the paste at the back to create a tiny 'Mexican hat'.

5. Moisten the inside of the calyx, and set the flower in place, very carefully pressing the throat of the flower against the calyx. Immediately mark the centre with a five-pointed veining tool.

6. Paint the flower centre with lemon paste colour, using a fine brush. Start with one fine line about one third of the way up the middle of each petal, then using tiny strokes, continue to paint a star pattern as shown.

7. Drop a tiny ball of pale green paste into the centre for the pistil.

BUDS

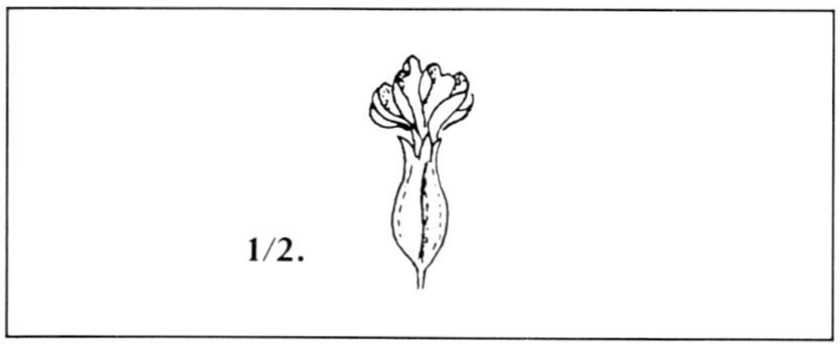

1. Prepare calyx as for the flower, but smaller.

2. Repeat the flower as above, but use a smaller cutter. When the petals are in place, lift them up so that they appear to be just opening.

3. For the tiniest buds, use two petals only from the smallest cutter. Thin and roll them up into a cigar, then push this down into the calyx as far as it will go.

PRIMROSE

LEAVES

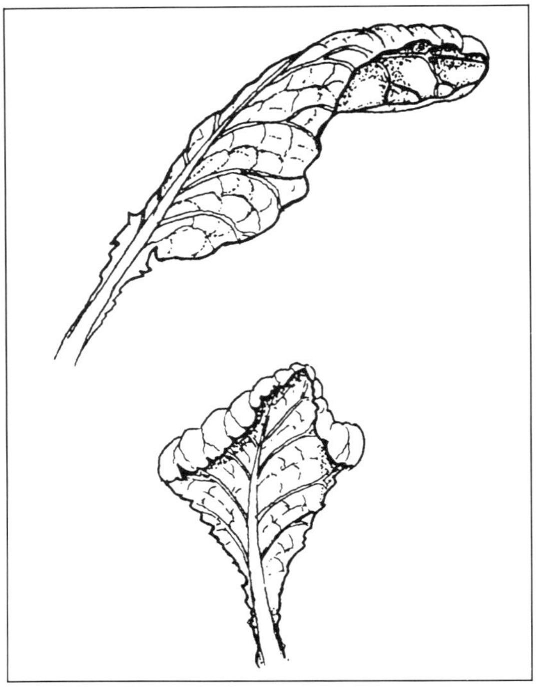

1. Colour flower paste a light fresh green, and cut out the leaves using the method shown on pages 10 and 11.

2. Take particular care to thin the edges really well, as they need to be curled under. Vein well on both sides.

3. Using powder colours and flat brushes, brush the young leaves with a slightly darker moss green over the central area, then brush lime green or yellow along the edges. Colour the lower central vein with a light rose pink.

4. Glaze with 'half glaze' and leave to dry for about five minutes. As soon as it is possible to handle the leaf, encourage the edges to curl under and curve the wire back.

5. When the leaf is thoroughly dry, colour the veins on the back with a flat brush and rose powder. NB: If you colour these veins before you glaze, you will probably lose the colour.

6. Some of the leaves may be changing colour. Start with the same light green, then brush on cream powder with a little brown on the edges.

ASSEMBLY

Several long-stemmed flowers grow from the centre of a rosette of leaves. Hold all the flowers together in one hand, then add the buds. The younger the bud, the shorter the stem. Bind securely with fine silver wire. Add the smallest leaves closest to the flowers, and the larger leaves outside. Wire in. Finally add the brown leaves so that they grow from underneath the green ones. Continue to bind down the stems, which may then be cut off to the length required. Tape over the wires with green stem tape.

When the arrangement is in place, pull the leaves down so that they fall softly onto the surface of the cake or the base. Curve the flower stalks.

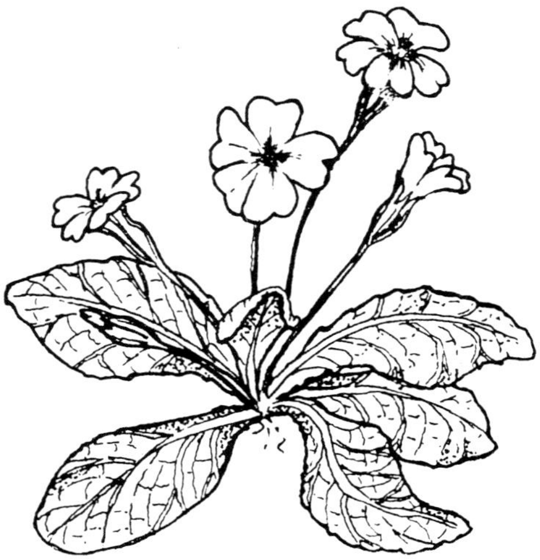

PRIMROSE

PUSSY WILLOW

The Springtime brings a lovely sight,
Pussy willow, silver bright.
Down woodland ways these silken flowers
Sparkle in the sudden showers.

Pussy Willow is the popular name for Goat Willow. The male catkins are often used to decorate churches on Palm Sunday. The twigs are very easy to make and add an unusual dimension to your Easter floral arrangements.

BUDS AND CATKINS

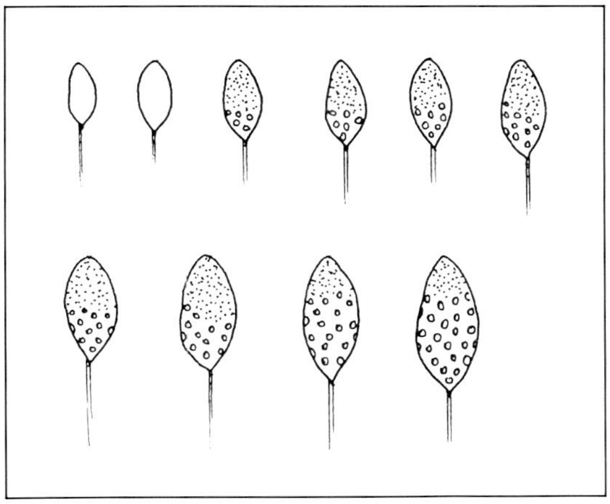

1. Make small oval balls in white paste on hooked 30 gauge wires, in a range of 9 to 12 sizes, as shown. Pinch a tiny point at the base. Squash with the fingers to flatten just a little.
Leave to dry thoroughly.

2. Brush the two smallest buds with Brilliant Silver powder colour.

3. Brush each of the other buds with egg white, then dip into white Sugar Tex to which brilliant silver powder colour has been added. Leave to dry.

4. Starting with the largest catkin, brush more egg white on the lower half and sprinkle with Mimosa Sugar Tex.

5. Repeat this on the next smaller catkins, but note that as the catkins get smaller, the area covered by the Mimosa Sugar Tex is reduced. Leave to dry.

CALYX

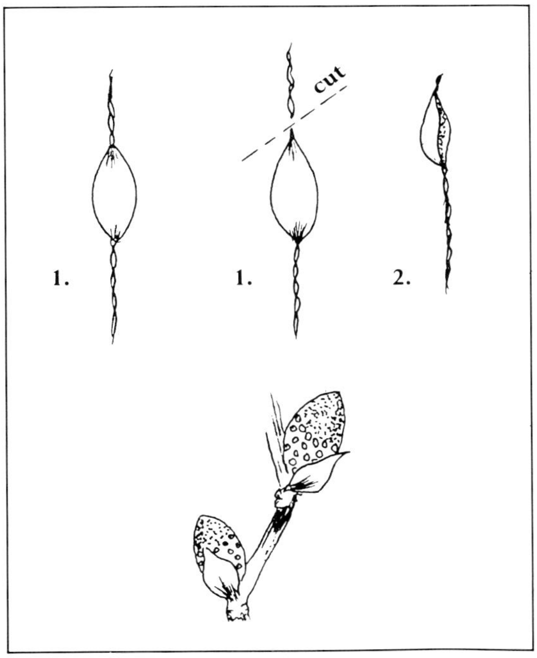

1. Cut short lengths of dark brown stem tape, and cut into half widths. Twist the tips very tightly, leave 1 cm ($^{2}/_{5}$ths inch) or less untwisted, then twist again down to the end. Cut off the tip.

2. Ball the centre of each one to cup.

3. Tape a calyx beside each bud or catkin, with dark brown quarter-width tape, and continue to tape down the wire for about 2½ cms (1 inch), keeping the tape very neat.

4. Using neat dark brown paste colour, paint the catkin where the paste and the tape meet.

ASSEMBLY

1. Tape the smallest bud to a 24 gauge wire using Twig stem tape. Leave no stalk.

2. Tape down the wire for about 1 cm ($^2/_5$ths inch), then add another bud and tape down for about 12 mm (½ inch).

3. Continue in this way, taping in the catkins as illustrated. As they get larger, so the space between the catkins is longer. Note that the buds and catkins appear to spiral round the twig, though it is difficult to find any precise pattern to their growth.

4. Bend the twig very slightly away from each bud or catkin.

5. With a large needle or the back of a pair of scissor blades, 'polish' all the twigs very vigorously, until they shine.

PUSSY WILLOW

VIBERNUM

Awaken to this golden morning
Senses stir to scent and sight,
Vibernums in the bird-song dawning
Catch and hold their own starlight.

This is one of the earliest blossoms to be found. A very pretty shrub with tiny buds and white flowers tinged with pink, which grow in small clusters. The flowers contrast beautifully with the brown twigs and fresh young leaves.

BUDS

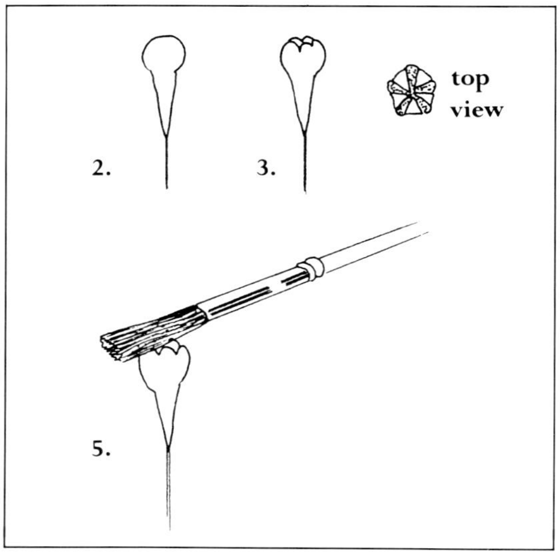

1. Make very small closed hooks on 33 gauge wire.

2. With white flower paste, roll a very small 'tadpole' shape. Insert the hooked wire from the 'tail' end and neaten.

3. With fine tweezers, pinch five small ridges into the 'head'.

4. Gently roll just below the 'head' between the two forefingers, to emphasise the shape.

5. Using a flat brush and pink powder colour, brush across the ridges at right angles, so that the colour is only picked up on the ridges and leaving the indents white. Also brush pink on to the stem.

6. Leave to dry.

FLOWERS

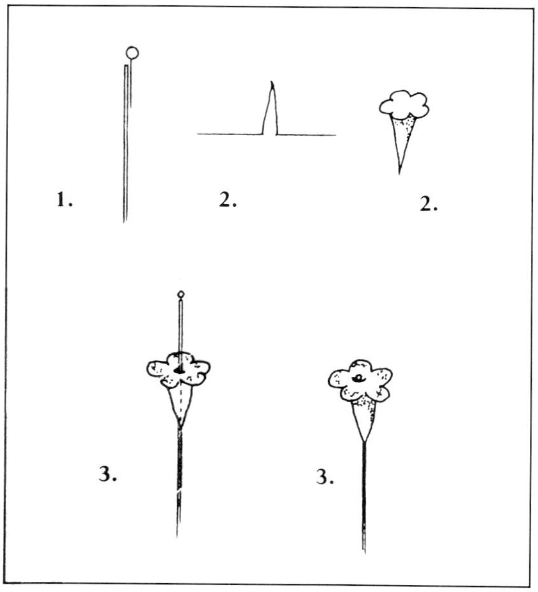

1. Attach one very small yellow stamen to the tip of a 30 gauge white wire with as little tape as possible. Try not to take the tape down the wire.

2. Using white flower paste, make a *very* small slim Mexican hat and cut out the smallest blossom with FMM B1 cutter. Thin the edges, making the petals look soft and slightly 'crumpled' rather than fluted.

3. Make a small hole right through the centre of the flower, with a needle, and pull through the stamen until the head just shows and does not protrude.

4. Leave to dry.

5. Brush with pink powder colour on the back of the flower and on the stem only.

VIBERNUM

LEAVES

1. Colour flower paste a light fresh green. Use very small and medium sized plain round leaf cutters, and vibernum leaf veiners.
NOTE: The younger the leaf, the more pronounced will be the veins. Make your veiner from a real leaf if possible.

2. Follow the instructions on pages 10 and 11.

3. Brush on just a hint of shadow green at the lower point, and Squires Kitchen Vine green on the top edges to emphasise the freshness of a very young leaf.

ASSEMBLY

1. Using quarter-width dark brown tape, put together small groups of five or six buds for the tip of the twigs.

2. Twist the tape tightly as you bind it several times on the same spot, to make a small thick band.

3. Roughen the surface of the thick band with a strong needle or scribe.

4. Continue to tape down the wires. Do not cut away any of the wires as you need them to thicken the twig.

5. 'Polish' the twigs until smooth and shiny, by rubbing them vigorously with the back of a pair of scissor blades or a large needle.

6. Tape together pairs of very small leaves, creating a small 'knot' as for the buds above.

7. Tape these to the main twig, then tape and polish for a few cms (about 1 inch).

8. Make further clusters with two or three buds on the inside, surrounded by up to five open flowers.

9. Create the knots as before, tape to the main twig and polish.

10. Some of the twigs may be made up of pairs of leaves only. Follow the illustration or a real example if possible.

VIBERNUM

RECIPES

FLOWER PASTE — RECIPE 1. KENWOOD MIXER

1 lb Icing sugar
3 rounded teaspoons Gum Tragacanth or Super Wernets Denture Fixative
5 teaspoons cold water
2 Rounded teaspoons white fat (trex)
2 rounded teaspoons liquid glucose
Size 3 egg white (lightly beaten)
2 level teaspoons Gelatine.

Method Place the Icing sugar and Gum Tragacanth or Super Wernets into an oven-proof mixing bowl. Place a sheet of kitchen towel and then a plate on top, with the dough hook on top of the plate.

Place into a very slightly warm oven (¼ Reg gas, 100C elec) for at least half an hour.

In the meantime, sprinkle the gelatine onto the cold water in a small basin. Leave to sponge for half an hour.

Place the gelatine basin over a pan of boiling water. Do not let the basin touch the water. Stir until the gelatine is completely dissolved. Stir in the white fat and the liquid glucose, and stir until clear.

Remove the sugar from the oven and place on the mixer.

Immediately pour in the gelatine mixture and the lightly beaten egg white. Cover the bowl with a tea cloth and switch on to low until the mixture is all stirred together, then remove the teacloth and turn the mixer to high for about five minutes. The more you mix, the better the paste.

Place in a double plastic bag immediately, and store in the refrigerator for 24 hours.

FLOWER PASTE — RECIPE 2. TYLO POWDER

1 size 3 egg white
15 mls Tylo powder
1½ cups Icing sugar

Method Place egg white in a small bowl and beat lightly.

Using a plastic spatula, stir in about half of the icing sugar. Mix well.

Add the Tylo powder all at once, and mix very quickly, scraping every grain from the sides of the bowl.

Scoop the mixture to one side of the bowl and stand the spatula against it whilst you wash your hands.

Place the rest of the icing sugar on the work surface, then spoon the Tylo mixture into the centre. Knead in as much of the sugar as possible.

Smooth white fat over the hands and knead again.

Wrap Cling Film which has been lightly smeared with white fat. Put into a plastic bag and then into an airtight container.

Store in the refrigerator.

NOTE: This paste can be used immediately, but is better if kept for 24 hours. Add more sugar if required.